The Talents

Part One

The Talents

An Unauthorized Biography of The Famous Parable

Part One

Doris E. Miller

Wipf and Stock Publishers
Eugene, Oregon
2003

ISBN 1-59244-224-2

For additional copies, contact your local bookstore, or the publisher:

Wipf and Stock Publishers
199 West 8th Avenue, Suite 3
Eugene, OR 97401

www.wipfandstock.com

The Talents

Part One

Preface

This volume is Part One of a larger work which will carry the same name.

Chapter 1 of Part One explains how the book evolved as a reaction to Max Weber's essay *The Protestant Ethic and the Spirit of Capitalism*, and leads into my claim that that ethic, so far as capitalism is concerned, is based less on the factors Weber named than on Jesus' stewardship parables, particularly the Parable of the Talents. As time went on the parable took over my book and the Weber element all but disappeared, but vestiges of it remain in this chapter, and may be of interest to readers unfamiliar with that work.

Chapter 2 presents my theory that Jesus spent his unrecorded years as a steward rather than (as traditionally believed) a carpenter, and that is why so many of his parables deal with stewardly concerns.

Chapter 3 discusses the stewardship parables in general.

Chapter 4 analyzes the relationship between the Parable of the Talents and that of its supposed variant, The Pounds, and attempts a reconstruction of the original texts.

Part Two of this work, in progress, reviews the known interpretations of The Talents from the times of the early church to the present, with special emphasis on its place in the English-speaking world today.

It is generally supposed that once the symbolism of The Talents is explained the meaning of the story is self-evident, but the broad range of existing opinions as to its authenticity and interpretation and its relevance to the problems of our age disproves that supposition. Widely quoted and misquoted, the parable finds its way into issues not only of personal life but of education, sociology, law, medicine, ecology: any field where questions of duty and ethics must be faced. It is a lasting presence in the Western world.

I must express my gratitude to Robert E. Gould, who took time from his own work on place-name etiologies in the book of Genesis to read and comment on successive drafts of these pages, and who also first called my attention to the city of Sepphoris.

Abbreviations

The following abbreviations are used throughout this book.

Books of the New Testament

Matthew	Matt.	1 Timothy	1 Tim.
Mark	Mark	2 Timothy	2 Tim.
Luke	Luke	Titus	Titus
John	John	Philemon	Philem.
Acts of the Apostles	Acts	Hebrews	Heb.
Romans	Rom.	James	James
1 Corinthians	1 Cor.	1 Peter	1 Pet.
2 Corinthians	2 Cor.	2 Peter	2 Pet.
Galatians	Gal.	1 John	1 John
Ephesians	Eph.	2 John	2 John
Philippians	Phil.	3 John	3 John
Colossians	Col.	Jude	Jude
1 Thessalonians	1 Thess.	Revelation	Rev.
2 Thessalonians	2 Thess.		

Versions of the Bible

KJV	King James (or Authorized) Version
NEB	New English Bible
RSV	Revised Standard Version
NRSV	New Revised Standard Version

1
In Search of an Ethic

Weber's Essay

In the opening years of the twentieth century a German sociologist published a book that created a sensation among scholars in the fields of sociology, history, and religion and has been a focus of recurring controversy ever since. The sociologist was Max Weber and the book was his famous essay *The Protestant Ethic and the Spirit of Capitalism.*[1] English translations published in 1930 and 1958 made the work familiar in British and American academic circles, where it gave rise to an enormous literature of praise and dispraise, amplification and negation. To most of the American public, however, this erudite essay, written by a European scholar for other European scholars, was almost literally a closed book. Only the title, as a trendy and provocative phrase, was picked up by college groups, talk shows and political pundits, and eventually became familiar to the general public.

At some time in the 1970s the frequency of cynical allusions to a "Protestant ethic" that I, a Methodist, had never heard of, provoked me into finding and reading the book.

It is a fascinating work, even if you don't accept its basic thesis. Weber's immense learning and ability to bring in historic figures and cite specific examples, large and small, to bolster his arguments, keep it from being merely a dry, theoretical treatise; but it is not an "easy read." Chapter IV, especially, "The Religious Foundations of Worldly

Asceticism," demands more study than the average college student, still less the general reader, is likely to give it. For the only mildly inquiring mind, therefore, the easiest course is to give up the effort and accept a shortcut which runs more or less as follows:

> Protestants have historically tended, as societies, to be richer than Catholics. They got that way [so the story goes] by ceaseless hard work and frugality—principles instilled in them by their peculiar religious beliefs. But hard work and frugality are not especially lovable characteristics, and prosperity achieved by such methods is not to be desired. Most deplorable, by setting such a pace of acquisitive activity, Protestants have forced the whole world into the same mold—that of capitalism, which Weber, in a famous passage, likened to an "iron cage."[2]

Does this do justice to Weber's thesis? It comes pretty close.

But does Weber's thesis do justice to Protestant ethics?

No; it is a caricature, strongly biased, and according to an increasing number of critics, not well documented. The bias was not a religious one: Weber, though officially a Lutheran, had by his own admission little or no religious feeling, and his essay, while critical of Protestantism, does not recommend Catholicism or Marxism or any other alternative as a better system. It seems to have been inspired partly by his intellectual interest as a sociologist in the question of why modern capitalism had developed only in the Western world, and partly by his revulsion against what he saw as the soulless materialism of his time. When in the course of his studies he discovered that "in any country of mixed religious composition," as he put it, "business leaders and owners of capital, as well as the higher grades of skilled labour, and even more the higher technically and commercially trained personnel of modern enterprises, are overwhelmingly Protestant,"[3] he felt he was on to something important, which must be pursued.

His eventual conclusion was that modern capitalism and commercialism were, to a considerable extent, results of a specifically Western event, the Protestant Reformation of the sixteenth century.

Weber stated his case a century ago, and decades of study by other scholars have greatly dimmed its luster. Still more damaging, it has been "overtaken by events." When in the last years of the twentieth century many Communist countries discovered that Communism was the real "iron cage" and broke out of it into the turbulent freedom of capitalism, it shook the whole structure of his argument. The controversy has cooled, and a considerable reevaluation of the thesis is now taking place, but the image of the cold and grasping capitalist as the alter ego of the Protestant will linger as long as Weber's essay is studied, and probably longer.

Perhaps the issue is no longer important. Political and economic situations and attitudes toward capitalism have changed so much since the Berlin wall came down that it might seem pointless to open once more the questions posed by this somewhat dated work. Yet considering its place in the social history of the twentieth century and its importance to the subject of its inquiry—the Protestants of the world—I think it is worthwhile to examine it again, and to offer some insight from a different angle.

Is there in fact a specifically Protestant ethic—a theory or system of moral values—in addition to basic Christian beliefs, which influences a society in the direction of worldly success? And if so, what does it consist of?

Max Weber was not, of course, the first to ponder these questions. The greater prosperity of Protestant societies was an old subject by his time; Weber himself and many of his critics quote from authors going back almost to the Reformation on this subject. In addition to the incidental observations of travellers, merchants, statesmen, etc., there were serious studies of it, and needless to say, much controversy. When the theme of prosperity was examined in connection with such others as freedom, justice, tolerance, public spirit, education, health, and morality, Protestants generally came off very well. Weber obviously knew of these studies, as is clear from his notes, but he wasted no space in discussing them. He was fascinated by his own theory, which he pursued relentlessly and, one might say, recklessly, with the enthusiasm of one who has seen the glimmer of a new idea and grasps at every shred of possible evidence for it.

As an example of this method, here is a passage from the second chapter of *The Protestant Ethic*, in which he offers a "provisional description" of what he means by the spirit of capitalism. He takes it from a document which, he says, "contains what we are looking for in almost classical purity." The document is Benjamin Franklin's once familiar piece, "Advice to a Young Tradesman:"

> Remember that *time* is money. He that can earn ten shillings a day by his labor, and goes abroad, or sits idle, one half of the day, though he spends but sixpence during his diversion or idleness, ought not to reckon *that* the only expense; he had really spent, or rather thrown away, five shillings besides... Remember that *credit* is money... Remember that money is of the prolific, generating nature... [etc.].[4]

This is helpful advice addressed to a specific kind of person: a hard-working young artisan (Franklin speaks of "the sound of your hammer at five o'clock in the morning") who may have little conception of money management, or of its perils and possibilities. No one would consider it a guide to life as a whole. But Weber expands it into a "philosophy of avarice."

> Truly what is here preached [says Weber] is not simply a means of making one's way in the world, but a

> peculiar ethic... It is not mere business astuteness, that sort of thing is common enough, it is an ethos. *This* is the quality which interests us[5]... The *summum bonum* of this ethic, the earning of more and more money, combined with the strict avoidance of all spontaneous enjoyment of life... is thought of so purely as an end in itself that from the point of view of the happiness of, or utility to, the single individual, it appears entirely transcendent and absolutely irrational. Man is dominated by the making of money, by acquisition as the ultimate purpose of his life.[6]

Although Weber has introduced this as presenting the "spirit of capitalism," it is obvious that for him it could double as a description of the "Protestant ethic." In his last chapter, in fact, he calls attention to this:

> One has only to re-read the passage from Franklin, quoted at the beginning of this essay, in order to see that the essential elements of the attitude which was there called the spirit of capitalism are the same as what we have just shown to be the content of the Puritan worldly asceticism, only without the religious basis, which by Franklin's time had died away.[7]

Weber had chosen the most unlikely of examples. Franklin loved to give advice and dispensed it freely on many subjects without intending an "ethic": how to cure a smoking chimney, how to choose a wife (or a mistress), how to educate children, how to swim, how to play chess, etc. The implication that he preached or practiced an ethic that held up the making of money as the "ultimate purpose of life" ignores not only the content of his other writings but also the fact that he retired from business at the age of 42 to devote himself to broader interests and to become one of the most versatile Americans of his time: scientist, inventor, innovator, statesman, diplomat, philanthropist, public citizen. To connect him with the "strict avoidance of all spontaneous enjoyment of life" is equally absurd; he lived a long life, full of honors, did everything, knew everybody, and thoroughly enjoyed it all.

Anticipating, of course, many objections to his theory, Weber explains further what he means by capitalism. It is not simply greed: that is found everywhere and takes such various forms as wars of conquest, piracy, colonialism, tax-farming, speculation, usury, etc.

> Unlimited greed for gain is not in the least identical with capitalism, and is still less its spirit. Capitalism may even be identical with the restraint, or at least a rational tempering, of this irrational impulse. But capitalism is identical with the pursuit of profit, and forever *renewed* profit, by means of continuous, rational, capitalistic enterprise.[8]

As for Protestantism, he acquits the Reformers themselves of any wish to promote the "spirit of capitalism." They were interested in the salvation of the soul and that alone. Yet by a paradoxical process they did not foresee, their followers set in motion this "most fateful force in our modern life."[9]

The overall impression left by the book is that the Protestant ethic is precisely that expressed by the devastating statement quoted above: "Man is dominated by the making of money, by acquisition as the ultimate purpose of his life."

How did Weber arrive at this astonishing conclusion? By neglecting all aspects of Protestantism except the economic ones, and by tracing those back, as he thought, to two distinctive ideas: the concept of the calling and the doctrine of predestination.

The concept of the calling, "a life-task, a definite field in which to work," was characteristic of all Protestant denominations. Since they had no monasteries and frowned upon the kind of devotion that expressed itself in feasting, fasting, vigils and processions, the layman's zeal had to express itself as a Christian life within his daily work; his occupation became his "vocation." Luther thought the monastic life not only without value but actually selfish, while labor in a calling appeared to him as the outward expression of brotherly love.

> The only way of living acceptably to God [continues Weber, explaining that view] was not to surpass worldly morality in monastic asceticism, but solely through the fulfillment of the obligations imposed upon the individual by his position in the world. That was his calling.[10]

It applied to all classes of society.

Such teaching contributed greatly to the rise of capitalism by increasing the regularity and dependability of economic processes, and particularly by the creation of a large work force imbued with the idea that faithful work in one's calling fulfilled a religious obligation.

> With the consciousness of standing in the fullness of God's grace and being visibly blessed by Him, the bourgeois business man, as long as he remained within the bounds of formal correctness, as long as his moral conduct was spotless and the use to which he put his wealth was not objectionable, could follow his pecuniary interests as he would and feel that he was fulfilling a duty in doing so. The power of religious asceticism provided him in addition with sober, conscientious, and unusually industrious workmen, who clung to their work as to a life purpose willed by God.[11]

Max Weber, a famous workaholic himself, recognized the "obligation which the individual is supposed to feel and does feel towards the content of his professional activity, no matter in what it consists,"[12] but he saw the mass of Protestant workers as—to put it bluntly—earnest stooges in the capitalist system.

As long as the book remained largely in the realms of academe, most Protestants, unfamiliar with its thesis, found the term "Protestant ethic" somewhat puzzling, but tended to assume it meant something good. In fact, as William Safire has noted, "In one of those quirks of semantic history, the 'Protestant ethic' soon lost the pejorative connotation Weber intended for it and acquired the sincere, hard-working positive connotation to people who believed in free enterprise and the development of individual character."[13] Below is a frank expression of the existing confusion, published in a letter to the editor of the Baltimore *Sun* in June, 1979:

> Sir:
> Richard H. Gilluly's May 28 op-ed page article, "New Authoritarians," intrigues me.
>
> I am not particularly hostile to encounter groups, but being a Presbyterian minister I should appreciate Mr. Gilluly's telling us more about "the Protestant ethic," which heads his list of those abominations ("rigidly authoritarian schools... subjugation of women" etc.) which he regards both as potentially the main cause of "the crime and delinquency, the family strife... the coldly bureaucratic and unresponsive institutions," and as "peculiarities of industrial civilization," by a logic which escapes me.
>
> How would Mr. Gilluly distinguish "the Protestant ethic" from the "Catholic" or the "Jewish" ethic? Or, from Platonic or Aristotelian, Epicurean, Stoic,

> Utilitarian or Marxist ethic? What is it that makes the Protestant ethic uniquely reprehensible?
>
> What, more precisely and specifically than was expressed in this article, is bugging Mr. Gilluly?
>
> —Ian Wilson, Baltimore[14]

And soon, inevitably, a second issue raised its ugly head. It may have started with President Nixon's Labor Day speech in 1971, praising the dignity of work and the "work ethic" as opposed to the "welfare ethic." The speech had no religious connotations, but in the press the "work ethic" and the "Protestant ethic" soon coalesced to form the "Protestant work ethic": a phrase never used, so far as I know, either in Weber's book or in the president's speech, but one that became and has remained, to many people, fighting words.

The following exchange appeared in Ann Landers' newspaper column in 1983, following a letter that bemoaned the decline of the "Protestant work ethic" and her sympathetic reply as to the value of work:

> Dear Ann Landers:
> I certainly agree with the person who complained about employees who take advantage by doing personal chores, writing letters and telephoning friends and relatives on company time. But I deeply resent your terminology. Why did you refer to it as the "Protestant work ethic"? Do you actually believe that Protestants work harder or are more ethical than Catholics and Jews?
>
> Many Catholics and Jews came to this country penniless, with little more than the clothes on their backs. They worked diligently and taught their children to do the same. They made this country what it

is today. Will you kindly explain why you used that phrase?

—O'Malley and Ginsburg in the Bronx

Dear O'Malley and Ginsburg:
The phrase "Protestant work ethic" is not original with me. It refers to the teachings of John Calvin (1509-1564), the French Protestant theologian. He taught that thrift, industry, sobriety and responsibility were essential to achieving the reign of God on earth. From this basic concept came "the Protestant work ethic." It certainly applies to people of all faiths.[15]

Dear Ann Landers:
Your response to O'Malley and Ginsburg was all right considering that the individual had never heard of the Protestant work ethic, but I disagree with your statement that it applies to people of all faiths.

There is, in fact, a Catholic work ethic (among others) which is specifically different from its Protestant counterpart. Space is at a premium, so a brief but powerful example will have to suffice.

Someone once asked Mother Teresa how she could continue to work so hard, knowing in her heart that there is no real chance of succeeding in her fight against poverty. Her answer: "We are not called to be successful; we are called to be faithful."

The Protestant work ethic has always held out the promise of material success as the reward for a job well done, whereas Catholicism tends to view work as

> a means to spiritual authenticity. This is why Protestantism was closely allied with the rise of capitalism, while Catholicism and capitalism are mortal enemies. No name, please. I have to live in this town.
>
> —Kalamazoo
>
> Dear Mazoo:
>
> You say the Protestant work ethic has always held out the promise of material reward for a job well done. How then do you explain the thousands of Protestant missionaries who, through the centuries, have labored among the impoverished in China, Japan and South America and trekked through the steaming jungles of Africa? As for Catholics being mortal enemies of capitalism, surely you jest. Many of the heaviest financial hitters in America are Catholics. For example: William E. Simon, chairman of Wesray; David Mahoney, former chairman of Norton Simon; James E. Burke, chairman of Johnson & Johnson; Thomas A. Murphy, former chairman of General Motors, to name a few.
>
> This great melting pot is composed of immigrants who came here in search of opportunity. They are people of every conceivable religious persuasion. You can be sure that no Catholic ever felt guilty for getting rich. Nor should he.[16]

Ann Landers soon curtailed the debate in her column, but resentment at the phrase is still warm, and does not cool.

The other major idea upon which Weber built his theory was the doctrine of predestination, supported chiefly by the Calvinists.

According to that doctrine, developed by St. Augustine and brought over by Calvin when he converted from Catholicism, every human being has been destined from before the creation of the world to eternal life or eternal damnation, and no act or belief of his own can change his fate. This is the "dreadful decree," disagreement over which has divided Protestant churches over the years.

Since according to this teaching God knows everything, including the future, he knows who will be saved and who damned. This must mean that it has all been determined in advance, and is unchangeable. For those who accepted the doctrine, the uncertainty over one's fate and the conviction that one could do nothing to alter it must have been an intolerable burden to carry through life. Such believers lived in fear of a hell to which, they supposed, most of mankind were doomed; but, searching for some ray of hope, some gleam of assurance, many Calvinists developed the idea that one could find signs of "election" in one's conduct. Only one of the elect, they reasoned, is able to augment the glory of God by his works. By leading irreproachable lives they increased the glory of God in the world, and by achieving success in their worldly endeavors they further increased that glory; and this could be taken to mean that God had *already*, from ages before, elected them to salvation. "Thus, however useless good works might be as a means of attaining salvation," says Weber, "… nevertheless they are indispensable as a sign of election."[17] That was the source of the Puritan "drive."

This part of the thesis has drawn heavy criticism, on the grounds that Weber gave it disproportionate emphasis. The majority of Protestants were not believers in predestination, so they could not have been moved by that reasoning, yet Protestants of all schools prospered, at varying rates: Calvinists, Arminians, Huguenots, Lutherans, Pietists, Presbyterians, the English with their national church, the Americans with their medley of free churches. Weber's explanation cannot be stretched to cover all of these.

The United States is a particularly interesting case. Weber thought it a prime example of the "capitalist spirit," but never realized how different the religious climate here was from that in Europe. He visited this country in 1904, observing American life, including religious life, with the keenest interest, but he did not apparently recognize that difference, with its greatly diminished knowledge of Luther and Calvin.

Paul Tillich did:

> The kind of Protestantism which has developed in America is not so much an expression of the Reformation, but has more to do with the so-called Evangelical Radicals. There are the Lutheran and Calvinist groups, and they are strong, but they have adapted themselves to an astonishing degree to the climate of American Protestantism. This climate has been made not by them but by the sectarian movements. Thus, when I came to America twenty years ago [1933], the theology of the Reformation was almost unknown in Union Theological Seminary, because of the different traditions, and the reduction of the Protestant tradition nearer to the non-Reformation tradition.[18]

By the "Evangelical Radicals" and the "non-Reformation tradition" Tillich means the Baptists, Congregationalists, Mennonites, Methodists, Quakers, Unitarians—in fact any Protestant church or sect not officially connected with one of the two great movements of the Reformation era in Europe, that is, Lutheran or Reformed (Calvinist). As to the Church of England, the third member of the "magisterial Reformation," it is difficult to think of that stately church as "radical," but it was certainly not tied closely to Calvin, and other American groups who were offshoots of the Church of England, or rebels against it, were similarly independent.

To many Protestants, therefore, Calvin was simply a revered name in history, and his doctrines seemed quite remote. For guidance in daily living they and their leaders went directly to the Bible. There among the parables of Jesus were many stories on stewardship which entered deeply into Protestant thinking: The Talents, The Pounds, The Laborers in the Vineyard, The Faithful and Wise Steward, The Unmerciful Servant, The Unjust Steward, The Wicked Husbandmen.

Of these, The Talents is the best known, the most broadly interpreted, and the most influential. To speak of a "Protestant ethic" without reference to The Talents is to leave out one of the pillars of the ethic. For centuries, children learned it in Sunday School, students were belabored with it at Commencement, the middle-aged measured their lives against it, and the dead were, whenever possible, eulogized with it.

It was not, of course, exclusively a Protestant possession. It speaks to all Christians. "We heard the parables," says a Catholic friend, speaking of her childhood. "They were read at Mass, in the pericopes. But we didn't have sermons on them." Protestants did have sermons on them, to the point where the preacher would sometimes feel compelled to apologize for bringing up a favorite tale once more.

And the more I read about the supposed "Protestant ethic," the more amazed I was that no one—neither Weber nor his critics—mentioned this bedrock teaching or gave it any weight in the formation of the Protestant character.

How could Weber, while quoting Calvin and Baxter and Spener, have overlooked the teacher of them all? For every Christian who has read the words of those men, thousands have read and memorized the words of Jesus. But Weber ignored that fact, partly, no doubt, because the Reformation, which divided Protestants and Catholics and sent them on their separate ways in so many respects, must have seemed the logical point at which to start his analysis, and partly because he thought of Jesus as a "semi-rural artisan" whose words could have no bearing on economic matters.[19] He mentions him by name only once in his famous essay, when he says,

> The personal attitude of Jesus is characterized in classical purity by the typical antique-Oriental plea: "Give us this day our daily bread." The element of radical repudiation of the world, as expressed in the *mamonas tes adikias* ["unrighteous mammon"], excluded the possibility that the modern idea of a calling should be based on his personal authority.[20]

In other words, the idea of the "calling" and the economic impetus it provided could not have come from Jesus himself because Jesus had no interest in the affairs of this world, taught his followers to be satisfied with a very simple standard of living, and considered wealth ("mammon") to be evil.

That would be a reasonable conclusion if one had only the phrases quoted above to go on, but if one considers Jesus' teachings as a whole the picture is quite different. Jesus did not repudiate the world—not, at least, as John the Baptist did. "John came neither eating nor drinking, and they say, 'He has a demon'; the Son of man came eating and drinking, and they say, 'Behold a glutton and a drunkard, a friend of tax collectors and sinners!'" (Matt.11:18,19) And he taught stewardship, the stewardship of God's gifts, through parables which used as their earthly symbols the management of wealth and property for the benefit of the owner. When he condemned the sharecroppers who held back the harvest and the steward who made no profit, he was asking for results, and results of a specific kind: a return on God's investment in mankind. The apostle Paul explained the fruits of the spirit as love, joy, peace, patience, kindness, goodness, faithfulness, gentleness, and self control, and this is surely the kind of fruit, or profit, that Jesus had in mind. It was probably inevitable, however, that it would also be interpreted as a call for the most productive and beneficial use, in this world, of whatever has been bestowed on us.

Jesus taught stewardship not merely as caretaking, but in the active, expansive sense of increase and improvement, of *profitable management*. There is in fact a clear capitalistic analogy in his parables. It is most vividly expressed in the Parable of the Talents, in which the "unprofitable servant" is cast into outer darkness while the successful ones are praised and promoted, but that is only one of many stories in which (as we suppose) God is presented as owner and master, and mankind as his stewards.

The wealth to which Jesus referred was (again as we suppose) spiritual wealth. Paul said, "This is how one should regard us, as servants of Christ and *stewards of the mysteries of God*" (I Cor.4:1). But for the average earth-bound mind this is hard to fathom, and for many centuries Christian stewardship has been most readily taken to mean the dedication to God of whatever means and opportunities we have: our time, our abilities, and our possessions, or in the well-worn phrase, "time, talent, and treasure."

Among the stewardship parables, that of the Talents is surely the best known. Its name, at least, is familiar even to people who know nothing of its origin and for whom it might as well be out of Aesop's fables or Poor Richard's Almanac. In this story, they know, three men receive from their master sums of money (talents) with which to work in his absence. The sums are very unequal, and this supposedly symbolizes the mystery and the basic unfairness of life. How the story continues they are not always certain, and the result is that the "talents" often lose their significance, and so does the story. The talents were not "gifts," as they are so often called; they were not a matter of careless generosity or mysterious favoritism; they were *venture capital*, advanced with the understanding that they would eventually be repaid, and if possible, with a profit.

Weber mentions the parable only once in *The Protestant Ethic*. In discussing the Puritan attitude toward the acquisition of wealth, he says that as a performance of duty in a calling, such acquisition was considered "not only morally permissible, but actually enjoined. The parable of the servant who was rejected because he did not increase the talent which was entrusted to him seemed to say so directly."[21] This implies that the Puritans read the parable as referring to actual wealth, whereas in fact they were keenly aware of its symbolism and of the austere judgement with which it ends.

THE PARABLE OF THE TALENTS (KING JAMES VERSION)

Here is the text of the parable, which I give first in the words of the King James (or Authorized) Version, because it is in this form that it has been engraved upon the minds of English-speaking people for more than three centuries, and it is in this form that it is most often quoted in our literature:

> The kingdom of heaven is as a man travelling into a far country who called his own servants, and delivered unto them his goods. And unto one he gave five talents, to another two, and to another one; to every man according to his several ability, and straightway took his journey.
>
> Then he that had received the five talents went and traded with the same, and made them other five talents. And likewise he that had received two, he also gained another two. But he that had received one went and digged in the earth, and hid his lord's money.
>
> After a long time the lord of those servants cometh, and reckoneth with them.
>
> And so he that had received five talents came and

brought other five talents, saying, Lord, thou deliveredst unto me five talents: behold, I have gained beside them five talents more. His lord said unto him, Well done, thou good and faithful servant: thou has been faithful over a few things, I will make thee ruler over many things: enter thou into the joy of thy lord.

He also that had received two talents came and said, Lord, thou deliveredst unto me two talents: behold, I have gained two other talents beside them. His lord said unto him, Well done, good and faithful servant; thou hast been faithful over a few things, I will make thee ruler over many things: enter thou into the joy of thy lord.

Then he which had received the one talent came and said, Lord, I knew thee that thou art an hard man, reaping where thou hast not sown, and gathering where thou hast not strawed: And I was afraid, and went and hid thy talent in the earth: lo, there thou hast that is thine.

His lord answered and said unto him, Thou wicked and slothful servant, thou knewest that I reap where I sowed not, and gather where I have not strawed: Thou oughtest therefore to have put my money to the exchangers, and then at my coming I should have received mine own with usury.

Take therefore the talent from him, and give it unto him which hath ten talents. For unto every one that hath shall be given, and he shall have abundance; but from him that hath not shall be taken away even that

> which he hath. And cast ye the unprofitable servant into outer darkness: there shall be weeping and gnashing of teeth. (Matt. 25:14-30)

The text is discussed in detail in Chapter 4, but a few notes here may be helpful:

Servants: In the Greek text of the New Testament, the word *doulos* may denote anyone working at the orders of a superior. The "servants" in this case appear to be white-collar employees. *Talent:* a very large sum of money, exact value impossible to state. *Several ability:* individual ability. *Straightway:* immediately. *Strawed:* strewn, as in winnowing, to separate grain from chaff. *Exchangers:* money-changers, who were often also bankers. *Usury:* interest. *Unprofitable:* some translations give "useless" or "worthless."

The Parable of The Talents (Revised Standard Version)

> For it will be as when a man going on a journey called his servants and entrusted to them his property; to one he gave five talents, to another two, to another one, to each according to his ability. Then he went away.
>
> He who had received the five talents went at once and traded with them; and he made five talents more.
>
> So, also, he who had the two talents made two talents more.
>
> But he who had received the one talent went and dug in the ground and hid his master's money.
>
> Now after a long time the master of those servants came and settled accounts with them.

And he who had received the five talents came forward, bringing five talents more, saying, "Master, you delivered to me five talents; here I have made five talents more."

His master said to him, "Well done, good and faithful servant; you have been faithful over a little, I will set you over much; enter into the joy of your master."

And he also who had the two talents came forward, saying, "Master, you delivered to me two talents; here I have made two talents more."

His master said to him, "Well done, good and faithful servant; you have been faithful over a little, I will set you over much; enter into the joy of your master."

He also who had received the one talent came forward, saying, "Master, I knew you to be a hard man, reaping where you did not sow, and gathering where you did not winnow; so I was afraid, and I went and hid your talent in the ground. Here you have what is yours."

But his master answered him, "You wicked and slothful servant! You knew that I reap where I have not sowed, and gather where I have not winnowed? Then you ought to have invested my money with the bankers, and at my coming I should have received what was my own with interest.

So take the talent from him, and give it to him who has the ten talents. For to every one who has will more be given, and he will have abundance; but from him who has not, even what he has will be taken away.

> And cast the worthless servant into the outer darkness; there men will weep and gnash their teeth" (Matt. 25:14-30).

What do the talents represent, and what are we to do with them? It is a question that has perplexed Christians for two thousand years and continues to haunt the thoughtful mind. The early Protestants took it with the utmost earnestness; they seldom mentioned the talents without, in the same breath, mentioning the Last Judgement and the rendering of accounts. John Milton wrote:

> He who hath obtain'd in more than the scantest measure to know anything distinctly of God, and of his true worship... remembring also that God even to a strictnesse requires the improvement of these his entrusted gifts, cannot but sustain a sorer burden of mind, and more pressing than any supportable toil, or waight, which the body can labour under; how and in what manner he shall dispose and employ those summes of knowledge and illumination, which God hath sent him into this world to trade with.[22]

Milton felt that his talent was that of scholarship, and if he was uncertain as a young man how best to use his abilities, he faced a still more difficult problem when in middle age he found himself going blind, and "that one talent which is death to hide" lodged with him—as he thought—useless.[23]

But the lesson was applied in every field. Henry Jeanes, quoted by Cotton Mather, urges public service as the proper use of the talent for some:

> The world applauds the politic retiredness of those that bury their parts and gifts in an obscure privacy, though both from God and man they have a fair call

> to public employment; but the terrible censure of these men by Christ at the last day will discover them to be the arrantest fools that ever were upon the face of the earth.[24]

Richard Steele writes, in *The Tradesman's Calling*:

> [Some] persons are equally unmindful of any temporal calling: that is, they no way promote the good of mankind; they have parts, but improve no science with them; have strength and health, but use no art or faculty; talents, but hide them in a napkin. O how will these give account to the judge of quick and dead?[25]

Susannah Wesley, writing to her husband, defended her practice of leading family worship in his absence:

> As I am a woman, so I am also mistress of a large family… in your absence I cannot but look upon every soul you leave under my care as a talent committed to me under a trust by the great Lord of all the families of heaven and earth. And if I am unfaithful to Him, or to you, how shall I answer when He shall command me to render an account of my stewardship?[26]

And William Blake wrote of his art:

> I am under the direction of messengers from Heaven, daily and nightly:… "If you, who are are organized by divine Providence for spiritual communion, refuse, and bury your talent in the earth… sorrow and desperation pursues you through life, and after death, shame and confusion of face, to eternity."[27]

This earnest attention to Jesus' activist teachings, which was shared to some extent by all levels of the population, is, I believe, the element that gives the "Protestant ethic" its dynamic character. The talents are seen as assets, abilities, or advantages of any kind which can be used to increase the glory of God and the happiness of mankind; and the man or woman who makes no use of them is the pitiful soul who will be "cast out."

Anyone who has grown up with the story as part of his religious heritage carries it with him forever. It may fade in and out of our consciousness as we cope with the problems of the here and now, but in thoughtful hours, as we try to make sense of our lives, it returns to confront us. There is much in our lives that we cannot control, yet—we are taught—some few talents were put directly into our hands. What were those talents, and what have we done with them?

Millions of people have pondered these questions, and the matter of judgement. What did *they* think? How did they work it out?

I began to search for answers, and was surprised to find how scattered the sources were: sermons, commentaries, theses, speeches, critical notes in religious journals, letters, memoirs, anecdotes… but so far as I could find, no attempt at a consecutive story reaching to the present. And I resolved to compile one.

With no scholarly credentials in this field, no favorite theory to support, I set out on an independent journey of exploration. The record is doomed to be incomplete and at times, perhaps, incorrect; but I found the journey a rewarding one, and I hope it will prove to be so as well for those who choose to retrace it with me.

2
Jesus the Steward

The Silent Years

For some two thousand years Jesus has been known as "the Carpenter of Nazareth," yet there has been recurrent speculation as to whether that phrase tells the whole story of his early life. Between his visit to the Temple at the age of twelve and the beginning of his ministry when he was "about thirty," there is a gap which conservative opinion has concluded cannot be filled. From time to time creative minds have floated theories that during those years he was living with the Essene sect, studying to be a rabbi, travelling in Tibet, learning magic in Egypt, and so on, but most scholars have accepted the traditional picture of him as a village craftsman, biding his time in the fragrant obscurity of a carpenter's shop. No one, to my knowledge, has made the suggestion—which seems so likely from the internal evidence—that he spent much of that time as a steward on a prosperous estate somewhere in Galilee.

I did not set out originally to study Jesus' life, but as I thought over the parable of the Talents it struck me again and again what a strange theme Jesus had chosen to convey his message. What other religious teacher asked you to show a profit on your life? Who else used so many monetary symbols, talked so frankly of debts, of profit and loss? The parable of the Talents is only one example of this interest; there are many others, and they comprise striking evidence in favor of Jesus' having been a steward, routinely involved in such matters.

I began to list the parables which have to do with wealth or with the care of property, in one form or another. Money and property are, of course, matters of interest to most of us, and at fund-raising times ministers and financial officers like to startle their hearers with the somewhat exaggerated statement that "half of Jesus' parables deal with money." The fund-raising over and the totals in, the statement is forgotten until the next such occasion, but it deserves more attention.

Why should Jesus have told so many stories about worldly goods? He came from a poor family, we believe, and surely he knew the problems of the poor: making a living, putting food on the table, struggling with debt, trying to stay honest, scraping up the tax money, facing disability, providing for the children, and so on. Those are the problems of the poor, in every age.

But Jesus' "money parables" do not reflect those things. They reflect the problems of the rich, or at least the propertied: making a profit, collecting on debts, getting good tenants, hiring workers, firing incompetents, settling wage disputes, estimating construction costs, fighting theft, taking advantage of bargains. Why should a poor man, especially a poor man with a religious message to deliver, take this point of view?

The most likely reason, it would seem, is that he had formerly been the steward of a rich man, that it had been his charge to maintain and improve the estate, and that when he began to preach he chose to picture man's responsibility toward God in terms of a steward's responsibility to his employer, and to use images and incidents out of his own experience to paint that picture.

> *Steward:* 1. A man entrusted with the management of the household or estate of another; one employed to manage the domestic affairs, superintend the servants, collect the rents or income, keep the accounts, etc. 2. One who acts as supervisor or administrator,

as of finances and property, for another or others.[1]

Examining the parables and other figures of speech used by Jesus, one sees how many of them cluster around precisely these functions. One group deals with farming, as might be expected in a primarily agricultural economy; another with housekeeping and hospitality, and another with money and management. The rest, a more miscellaneous group, do not deal so directly with these themes but may be said to be at home in the same "scene."

Agriculture

Crop culture	The plowman (Luke 9:62)
	The sower (Matt.13:3-8, Mark 4:3-8, Luke 8:5-8)
	The seed growing secretly (Mark 4:26-29)
	The fields white for harvest (John 4:35)
Labor shortage	The laborers are few (Matt. 9:37, Luke 10:2)
	The sons to work in the vineyard (Matt. 21:28-31)
Sabotage	The wheat and the tares (Matt. 13:24-30)
Weather	Reading the weather signs (Matt. 16:2,3)
Grain measure	Pressed down, shaken together (Luke 6:38)
Productivity	The mustard seed (Matt.13:31,32; Mark 4:31,32; Luke 13:18,19)
	The barren fig tree (Luke 13:6-9)
	The budding fig tree (Luke 21:29-30)
	You will know them by their fruits (Matt. 7:16-20)
Animal husbandry	Sheep and goats (Matt. 25:32,33)
	Lost sheep (Matt. 18:12,13)
	Sheep without a shepherd (Matt. 9:36, Mark 6:34)
	Sheep know the shepherd's voice (John 10:3-5)

	Dogs, swine (no pearls before swine) (Matt. 7:6)
	The hen and her brood (Matt. 23:37, Luke 13:34)
Hauling	My yoke is easy, my burden light (Matt. 11:29,30)

Housekeeping and Hospitality

Cooking	Savorless salt (Matt. 5:13, Mark 9:50, Luke 14:34,35)
Lighting	Lamp is not set under a bushel (Matt.5:15)
Mending	New patches on old garments (Matt. 9:16, Mark 2:21, Luke 5:36)
Winemaking	New wine in old wineskins (Matt. 9:17, Mark 2:22, Luke 5:37)
Baking	Leaven hid in meal (Matt. 13:33)
Household staff	The servants left in charge (Mark 13:33-37)
	The faithful and wise steward (Matt. 24:45-47)
	The farmer and his man (Luke 17:7-10)
	The watchful servants (Luke 12:35-38)
	The servant in authority (Matt. 24:45-57, Luke 12:42,46)
	The servant of two masters (Matt. 6:24, Luke 16:13)
Hospitality	The great banquet (Luke 14:16-24)
	The marriage feast (Matt. 22:2-10)
	Places at table (Luke 14:8-10)
	The friend at midnight (Luke 11:5-8)
	Invite the poor to feast (Luke 14:12,13)
	Wise and foolish maidens (Matt. 25:1-12)

Money and Management

Trade	The talents (Matt. 25:14-30)

	The pounds (Luke 19:12-27)
Good buys	The treasure buried in the field (Matt. 13:44)
	The pearl of great price (Matt. 13:45,46)
Inventory	Treasures new and old (Matt. 13:52)
Deterioration	Moth and rust consume (Matt. 6:19-21)
A wage dispute	The laborers in the vineyard (Matt. 20:1-16)
Construction costs	The tower builder (Luke 14:28-30)
Construction sites	The two houses (Matt. 7:24-27, Luke 6:48,49)
Fraud	The unjust steward (Luke 16:1-9)
Trouble with tenants	The empty house (Matt. 12:43-45)
	The wicked husbandmen (Matt. 21:33-41, Mark 12:1-9, Luke 20:9-16)
Debts	The two debtors (Luke 7:41-43)
	The unmerciful servant (Matt. 18:23-34)
Theft	The thief (Matt. 24:43, Luke 11:21,22)
	The strong man's house broken into (Matt. 12:29, Mark 3:27, Luke 11:21,22)
	Thieves break in and steal (Matt. 6:19-21)
Litigation	The defendant (Matt. 5:25-26, Luke 12:57-59)

There are also, of course, many parables which do not belong to any of these groups, and among them are the two best-known and best-loved of all: The Good Samaritan (Luke 10:30-37—not properly a parable, but usually grouped with them) and The Prodigal Son (Luke 15:11-32). But even these belong to the same general kind of practical business world as the stewardship parables: the Samaritan is generally assumed to have been a merchant travelling a regular route, since he had credit with the innkeeper, and the prodigal son is involved in a division of family property.

It may seem that I have arranged the parables arbitrarily simply to make my point, and that other arrangements might bring out other patterns just as significant. Stewardship is a fairly broad concept, it is true, and accommodates many ideas. What brings out more sharply Jesus' concentration on this field, however, is a consideration of the themes he might have chosen—might have been *expected* to choose, for various reasons—and did not.

None of the parables, for instance, deals with carpentry. Of his figures of speech, the famous "mote and beam" (or "speck and log") (Matt. 7:3-5, Luke 6:41,42) may indeed hark back to the carpenter's trade but have essentially little to do with it. They are used only for the sake of a vivid, an exaggerated, contrast in size. "Why do you see the speck that is in your brother's eye, but do not notice the log that is in your own eye?" Many other images might have served just as well, and in fact, the gnat and the camel serve exactly the same purpose—grotesque contrast—in another of Jesus' sayings: "You blind guides, straining out a gnat and swallowing a camel" (Matt. 23:24). His promise, "My yoke is easy," though of course used figuratively, is often cited as a reflection of his trade since yokes were made of wood, but the full saying sounds more appropriate to the man who drives or leads the ox than to the carpenter, for it is, "My yoke is easy and my burden is light" (Matt. 11:30).

It is noteworthy, too, that though he is sometimes spoken of as a craftsman, he draws no images from the work of the craftsmen who would have been his neighbors in the village, and whose labors have inspired so many figures of speech: the potter, the weaver, and the smith. The world of Jesus' parables is not the village, nor is it the city, nor yet the family farm. It appears to be primarily the large estate, owned by a rich man, managed by stewards, and worked by tenants or hired labor.

Then, Jesus was a Galilean; he spent much time, it would seem from the gospels, on or near the Sea of Galilee; he preached from a boat, he walked on water, he stilled the storm. Capernaum, his base during most of his ministry, was a fishing town. His first four disciples were fishermen, and he told them, "I will make you fishers of men"

(Matt. 4:19). But after that, with a single exception (Matt.13: 47,48) he never mentioned fishing or boats, much less seamanship or seas. The thought so familiar to us of life as a voyage over stormy seas is entirely absent from his teaching. His images were land-based: vineyards, grain fields, sheep folds.

He lived in an occupied country that seethed with resentment and dreamed of empire, and he himself was accused of planning revolt, but (again with a single exception—Luke 14:31,32) he did not use military metaphor. It was the apostle Paul who talked about putting on the "armor of light" (or of God or of righteousness) and "fighting the good fight." A long succession of exhorters have appealed for "soldiers of the cross"; Jesus himself only asked for faithful and wise stewards.

Most surprising, perhaps, is that the parables do not mention healing. The analogy between physical and spiritual healing has been recognized at all times, and within Christianity it has been the basis of innumerable hymns, poems, and sermons. Jesus was a fabulously successful healer, and this was a great part of his popular appeal. "They brought him all the sick, those afflicted with various diseases and pains, demoniacs, epileptics, and paralytics, and he healed them. And great crowds followed him" (Matt. 4:24,25). He healed not for money or for popularity but out of compassion, and sometimes, it seemed, when he would have preferred to be teaching. So great was his reputation in that respect that two centuries after his death and after the separation between Christians and Jews, some Jews still surreptitiously invoked his name in healing.[2] Yet none of the parables involve healing, and when Jesus wanted a metaphor for the effect of God's grace upon man, he did not describe it as the remission of an illness, but as the remission of a debt.

It may be argued that since none of these themes, which were undoubtedly a part of his life, appear in his parables, it is not necessarily significant that he makes no reference to carpentry. It does not prove that he was not a carpenter, but merely that carpentry did not appeal to him as a preaching theme.

Time and again, however, he drew his stories from some aspect of stewardship. The simplest explanation is that he was indeed a steward, an *oikonomos*,[3] for much of his working life. How can that theory be harmonized with the longstanding tradition that he was a carpenter?

THE CARPENTER TRADITION

The tradition that Jesus was a carpenter hangs by a single thread: a single question asked when Jesus, in the course of his travels, came back to Nazareth and spoke in the synagogue there. He was first welcomed, then taunted by the townspeople. According to Mark the villagers asked each other, "Is not this the carpenter, the son of Mary and brother of James and Joses and Judas and Simon, and are not his sisters here with us?"(Mark 6:3) According to Matthew they asked, "Is not this the carpenter's son? Is not his mother called Mary? And are not his brothers James and Joseph and Simon and Judas?"(Matt.13:55,56) According to Luke they asked, "Is not this Joseph's son?"(Luke 4:22) The assumption has always been that these were rhetorical questions; everyone knew that he was a simple villager, like themselves, and they could not take him seriously as a teacher or a prophet. Where then, they asked, did this man get all this? "And they took offense at him" (Mark 6:2,3).

Was Jesus known in Nazareth as "the carpenter" or "the carpenter's son"? The question has not seemed important to most Christians, since trades were customarily handed down from father to son, and it might well have been that both Joseph and Jesus were carpenters; but in connection with this study it becomes important. If he was known as the carpenter, that effectively rules out the steward theory, but if he was known as the carpenter's son, then the question of his own occupation remains open.

Because Mark is considered the earliest of the gospels and thus closest to the sources, and also because this is the only apparent reference in the Bible to Jesus' worldly occupation, his version has become traditional; hence, "the carpenter of Nazareth." But that is not universally accepted.

The Interpreter's Bible argues for "the carpenter's son" as the original reading in all three gospels, on the grounds that if Mark had written "the carpenter," it is very unlikely that Matthew and Luke (both of whom used Mark as a source) would have changed it to "the son."[4] In several old and well-respected manuscripts, says this commentary, Mark's wording agrees with the others.

If we can assume, then, that in this incident Jesus was recognized only as the carpenter's son, that suggests that he had no identity of his own in the village. If he had lived there all his life he should not have needed to be identified by his father's name and occupation and the names of all his brothers. To me, this passage tends to corroborate other clues that Jesus had left Nazareth long before this—possibly as a "beardless boy"—and was returning as a virtual stranger. The villagers' questions sound less like slurs than simply efforts to recognize him, and to connect him with memories of a youth who had left the village years before.

The point is important, for it opens up space in his life for developing a different career. He might have gone away at age thirteen or fourteen. At that point he would have finished whatever schooling he was going to get; his parents—or his mother, possibly a widow by that time—had many other children to feed, and he, as the oldest son, would naturally have come forward to do what he could to help.

He had no doubt learned some carpentry from Joseph, but that trade, as practiced in Nazareth, seems not to have been a highly skilled or a very remunerative one. By Jesus' time Palestine had lost most of its forests and there was little wood available.The situation was similar to that described in 1939 by George Lamsa, a man who grew up in a country and in circumstances much like those in which Jesus lived, in spite of the passage of centuries.[5] Lamsa pointed out that in many

Eastern countries a "carpenter" is not—and especially in past times was not—a full-time craftsman. Village houses were usually built of stone or mud brick, by their owners. Because of poverty among the rural population there was little furniture, and even the yokes and plows—often assumed to be among the products of Jesus' trade—were usually made of branches cut from trees and shaped by the farmers themselves. The "carpenter," therefore, was simply one of the farmers who had a few tools and a little more skill than the others, and who was called on occasionally for special tasks. It was a trade with a very limited future—at least in Nazareth.

The gospels make no mention of Jesus leaving his home town until the beginning of his ministry, and then only in the briefest of terms. After describing the ministry of John the Baptist, Mark says merely, "In those days Jesus came from Nazareth of Galilee and was baptized by John in the Jordan" (Mark 1:9). After John's arrest "Jesus came into Galilee," and "passing along by the Sea of Galilee" he recruited his first four disciples and went on to Capernaum (Mark 1:14-21). Matthew's account, of course, is similar: "Then Jesus came from Galilee to the Jordan to John to be baptized by him" (Matt.3:13), and after John's death "he withdrew into Galilee, and leaving Nazareth he went and dwelt in Capernaum by the sea" (Matt.4:12,13). The two accounts, taken together, seem to bracket Jesus effectively into rustic Nazareth right up to the beginning of his ministry, leaving no possibility in his life for years of work as a steward.

But that conflicts with the impression given by his visit to the synagogue there. At that time, according to Luke, Jesus had been travelling widely through the surrounding country, and his visit to his home town was just one more stop in his travels. "He came to Nazareth, where he had been brought up," says Luke 4:16. The last clause sounds like a reference specifically to his childhood years; one does not usually speak of a man's "bringing up" as extending to his thirties.

Where were his family on that Sabbath day? Out of his four brothers was there no one in the synagogue to speak for him? Perhaps in those many unrecorded years his brothers had also left little Nazareth in search of greater opportunities, though the sisters, probably married to local men, still lived there. ("Are not his sisters here with us?") The sisters apparently represented the last connections of Jesus' family with the town.[6]

To me this incident confirms the likelihood that Jesus spent his childhood in Nazareth and his working youth elsewhere in Galilee.

Sooner or later, I believe, he must have set out, like millions of other small-town boys, in search of a better future for himself and the family at home. We have no clues as to where he went or what he planned, but Sepphoris, the provincial capital, would have been a logical place to start. It was close, it was rich, and it was in the middle of a building boom.

Sepphoris

Although Sepphoris was a famous city with a long history, and although it was within walking distance of Nazareth, it is not mentioned in the Bible and until recently has hardly been considered a part of Jesus' world.

An article in *Biblical Archaeology Review* for May/June 1992 states:

> Continuing archeological excavations here are yielding evidence of a sophisticated urban culture that places Jesus in a radically different environment, one that challenges traditional assumptions about his life and ministry. The popular picture of Jesus as a rustic growing up in the relative isolation of a small village of 400 people in the remote hills of Galilee must be integrated with the newly revealed setting of a burgeoning Greco-Roman metropolis boasting upwards

> of 30,000 inhabitants—Jews, Arabs, Greeks and Romans. Sepphoris—powerful, prosperous, peace-loving—was linked with other Greco-Roman centers on the trade routes of the Greek-speaking East.[7]

The city had been destroyed by the Romans as punishment for a revolt there after the death of Herod the Great, but it was almost immediately rebuilt by the son, Herod Antipas. For almost three decades following Jesus' birth, Sepphoris served as the capital of Galilee and Perea.

> When Antipas returned to Galilee from Rome in the spring of 3 B.C. he selected the smoldering ruins of Sepphoris for the location of his new capital. Centrally situated in Galilee, Sepphoris already had a long and impressive history as a seat of government. Antipas launched a vast construction project that lasted throughout the life of Jesus, who was born about 6 B.C. Sepphoris became the nerve center for the government's control of Galilee and Perea. Political policy, military strategy, economic regulation and cultural affairs were administered from this seat of power. Influences from Sepphoris affected the people living in Nazareth as well as other satellite villages. Josephus tells us that Sepphoris was the largest and most beautiful city in Galilee.[8]

The fact that the Gospels contain no mention of this capital city, so close to Nazareth, is remarkable. In his youth, and later, in his many travels over Galilee did Jesus never visit the big city? It is sometimes suggested that he might have avoided it because it was disliked by Jews as a symbol of the occupying power, but archeological evidence does not support that explanation. Eric M. Meyers, excavator of the city, says:

> While a distinctly Jewish town, Sepphoris was cosmopolitan and unlike many of its neighbors managed to forge a working relationship with Rome even after participating in two wars against the empire... The construction of buildings adorned with classic pagan motifs alongside other buildings with such quintessential Jewish elements as *miqva'ot* (ritual baths) which we have found in the earliest Roman strata through the Byzantine layers, indicates that the local Jewish population saw no conflict between a traditional Hebrew way of life and the gentile culture of the nascent Greco-Roman world.[9]

A city under construction, or reconstruction, would have had a constant need for builders. If Jesus as a youth did work at carpentry, therefore, he might have had a hand in the rebuilding of Sepphoris, but there is no indication that he did so. In any case, this would have been an ideal place for a boy to see "the world at work," to meet new people and try new trades, and to find a good employer as—to judge by his parables—he eventually did.

That he went to Sepphoris and that that was a turning point in his life is of course only a conjecture, and leads to similar conjectures. Did he find employment there? Or was his employer a landowner with a country estate, as many of the parables suggest? In the course of his duties, would he not have learned to speak Greek as a practical necessity? He had evidently learned to dine in the Roman fashion, reclining at table, as many scriptural passages indicate.[10] What else had he learned there? Did he find himself becoming too "assimilated," and was that part of what prompted him to seek out John, to be baptized?

Such speculation is hard to resist, but it does not belong in this book. Let me return to what we know of him from his own words.

"One Who Serves"

Jesus called himself "one who serves," and this is usually understood in a general sense, as referring, for instance, to one who serves humanity. But it may have been literal, as well. There is a famous passage in Philippians (Chapter 2:5-7) in which Paul exhorts the church at Philippi to be humble and unselfish: "Have this mind among yourselves, which is yours in Christ Jesus, who, though he was in the form of God, did not count equality with God a thing to be grasped, but emptied himself, taking the form of a servant, being born in the likeness of men."

"Servant" here is *doulos*, the word most commonly used in the gospels. It also means "slave." But there is another, less common word for servant, which Jesus frequently used in speaking of himself and in instructing his disciples. The noun is *diakonos*; the verb, *diakoneo*, which means to serve, but especially, to attend personally, to care for someone, as a servant, host, or friend; to "wait on," "to minister to." In the three synoptic gospels it is most often used to mean specifically serving food, as in the story of Mary and Martha, or in that of the farmhand who must first serve his master before he himself can eat, or the master who, coming home from the wedding feast, serves the servants who have waited up for him.[11] Jesus used the word often, among his disciples. "If anyone would be first, he must be last of all, and servant (*diakonos)* of all" (Mark 9:35, and similar statements in other gospels). "Even as the Son of man came not to be served, but to serve" (Matt. 20:28). In Luke's account of the Last Supper, Jesus asks his disciples, "Which is greater, one who sits at table, or one who serves? Is it not the one who sits at table? But I am among you as one who serves" (Luke 22:27). And in John's account, Jesus takes off his outer garments, ties a towel around his waist, and with a basin of water washes his disciples' feet (John 13:4-9).

Was this simply a dramatic way of making his point, or was he pointedly recalling his own humble beginnings?

His words had their effect—surely an unintended one. The apostles took him literally, and after his death they made themselves into waiters, serving the poor and their fellow Christians at community suppers until they began to feel that that was perhaps too strict an interpretation of his command. "The twelve summoned the body of the disciples and said, It is not right that we should give up preaching the word of God to serve tables" (Acts 6:2). So they asked for seven men to be appointed *diakonoi*, deacons, men who serve tables; and the apostles gave themselves to prayer, "and to the ministry (*diakonia*) of the word."

But if Jesus began as a menial servant he did not remain one.

There is an odd passage in Matthew in the course of which Jesus says, apparently speaking of himself, "If they have called the master of the house Beelzebul, how much more will they malign those of his household" (Matt. 10:25). Beelzebul or Beelzebub is of course a devil. The Greek word rendered in English as "master of the house" is *oikodespotes*. Most commentators seem to understand it here as simply a figurative term for "leader," but it may have a more pointed significance. The literal meaning is "despot (or dictator) of the house." According to Liddell and Scott's *Greek-English Lexicon* it can mean either the master or the steward.[12] Especially in the case of an absentee owner or a very important personage it would be the steward who gave the orders and actually governed the household staff from day to day (compare the term *majordomo,* "chief of the house"). In this case its application to Jesus might be contemporary evidence that he was well-known to have been a steward.

Two Stories From Life

I have based most of my stewardship theory on the contents of the parables, which are discussed in later chapters, but two incidents in

Jesus' ministry also have a connection with the subject.

Consider, first, the incident of the wedding at Cana.

> On the third day there was a marriage at Cana in Galilee, and the mother of Jesus was there; Jesus also was invited to the marriage, with his disciples. When the wine gave out, the mother of Jesus said to him, "They have no wine." And Jesus said to her, "O woman, what have you to do with me? My hour has not yet come." His mother said to the servants, "Do whatever he tells you." Now six stone jars were standing there, for the Jewish rites of purification, each holding twenty or thirty gallons. Jesus said to them, "Fill the jars with water." And they filled them up to the brim. He said to them, "Now draw some out, and take it to the steward of the feast." So they took it. When the steward of the feast tasted the water now become wine, and did not know where it came from (though the servants who had drawn the water knew), the steward of the feast called the bridegroom and said to him, "Every man serves the good wine first; and when men have drunk freely, then the poor wine; but you have kept the good wine until now" (John 2:1-10).

Did Jesus really change water into wine by miraculous means? While he was fasting in the wilderness he had refused to resort to miracles to relieve his own hunger, on the grounds that "you shall not tempt the Lord your God" (Luke 4:12). And what about Mary's behavior? She is concerned for the family of the host, but what does she expect Jesus to do about it? The conventional explanation is that she knew of his miraculous powers and saw nothing incongruous in asking him to use them for such a purpose. But if Jesus had been a professional steward Mary might quite naturally and sensibly have turned to him for advice, without expecting a miracle; he had "been around," he would know what to do or say in such a predicament.

We do not know how he solved the problem (it is often pointed out that turning that much water into wine would have produced its own problems); but a few years later, when he had become a legend and when every incident involving him was being remembered and retold, the wedding at Cana would have been recalled, and the toast-master's remark and the mysterious business with the water jars might easily have coalesced into the story of a miracle.

Another story with stewardly elements is the Feeding of the Multitudes, recorded in all the gospels. I give it here according to Matthew, though it leaves out many details mentioned by the others.

> Now when Jesus heard this, he withdrew from there in a boat to a lonely place apart. But when the crowds heard it, they followed him on foot from the towns. As he went ashore he saw a great throng; and he had compassion on them, and healed their sick. When it was evening the disciples came to him and said, "This is a lonely place, and the day is now over; send the crowds away to go into the villages and buy food for themselves." Jesus said, "They need not go away; you give them something to eat." They said to him, "We have only five loaves here and two fish." And he said, "Bring them here to me." Then he ordered the crowds to sit down on the grass; and taking the five loaves and the two fish he looked up to heaven, and blessed, and broke and gave the loaves to the disciples, and the disciples gave them to the crowds. And they all ate and were satisfied. And they took up twelve baskets full of the broken pieces left over. And

> those who ate were about five thousand men, besides women and children (Matt.14:13-21).

A number of commentators have suggested that Jesus simply persuaded people to share food with each other, using the five loaves and two fish (which according to the Gospel of John had been brought by a boy in the crowd) to start a share-the-food movement; it is unlikely, they note, that the boy was the only one who had brought something with him. Other scholars suggest that the whole thing never happened, but was told as a kind of parable of the "Messianic feast." Still others say the multitudes were surely fed, and by Jesus, but they point out that none of the gospels calls it a miracle, thus leaving open the whole question of where the food came from.

I have no new theory to offer; I am simply interested in Jesus' approach to the situation, which was very matter-of-fact. In John's account Jesus asks Philip, perhaps just to see what his reaction will be (perhaps he was joshing him a little), "How are we to buy bread, so that these people may eat?" and the sober Philip answers, "Two hundred denarii would not buy enough bread for each of them to get a little!" (John 6:5).

Jesus then instructs them to seat the people on the grass.

The Interpreter's Bible contains an interesting anecdote in the discussion of this story. It concerns the British Baptist missionary Timothy Richard, who served as a relief administrator in Chinese famines from 1876 to 1884. He found it impossible to distribute the food effectively because he could not hold back the milling crowds. "Till one day at morning worship he happened to read the verse [John 6:10] in which Christ said, 'Make the people sit down,' and at a flash he saw the way out of his problem and perplexities. Sitting people do not shove or crush!"[13]

Jesus not only had them sit down, he had them do so in "companies" or groups: Luke says by fifties (Luke 9:14), Mark, "by hundreds and by fifties" (Mark 6:40). The only apparent purposes of this would be, first, to reckon how many mouths he had to feed, and second, to permit efficient distribution of the food.

And when they had eaten their fill, he told his disciples, "Gather up the fragments left over, that nothing may be lost" (John 6:12).

Miraculous or not, it was very stewardly.

Stewardship in the Epistles

The words *oikonomos* (steward) and *oikonomia* (stewardship) occur nine times in the pastoral letters of Paul and his followers. These letters are presumed to be among the nearest sources in the New Testament to the actual lifetime of Jesus, and the importance they attach to stewardship strongly suggests that they reflect Jesus' own life and teaching.

Thus I Pet. 4:10 says, "As each has received a gift, employ it for one another, as good stewards of God's varied grace." Titus 1:7 has "A bishop, as God's steward, must be blameless." I Cor. 4:1,2 says "This is how one should regard us, as servants of Christ and stewards of the mysteries of God. Moreover, it is required of stewards that they be found trustworthy." All this is pretty straightforward.

Stewardship itself is another matter. Jesus told his stewardship parables in the most down-to-earth words, though obviously with a figurative meaning. Paul takes a cosmic approach. In his letters the word *oikonomia* becomes so lofty and so protean as almost to defy translation.

Below are four passages which illustrate the point. My interlinear New Testament[14] uses "stewardship" wherever *oikonomia* appears. The King James Version uses "stewardship" in the parables and "dispensation" in the pastoral letters. The Revised Standard Version renders it with a different word on each occurrence ("commission," "stewardship," "office," "plan").

I am entrusted with a *commission*... (I Cor. 9:17).

> … The *stewardship* of God's grace that was given to me for you, how the mystery was made known to me by revelation… (Eph. 3:2).
>
> … The divine *office* which was given to me for you, to make the word of God fully known, the mystery hidden for ages and generations… (Col. 1:25-26).
>
> He has made known to us in all wisdom and insight the mystery of his will, according to his purpose which he set forth in Christ as *a plan* for the fullness of time (Eph. 1:9,10).

The New English Bible has "trust," "gift," and "task" in the first three of these passages, and paraphrases the last.

Similarly, in the letter called First Timothy the writer counsels Timothy that his people should not "occupy themselves with myths and endless genealogies which promote speculations" but rather "the divine training that is in faith" (I Tim. 1:3,4). *Oikonomia*, here translated as "divine training," is rendered in the KJV as "godly edifying," and in the New English Bible as "God's plan" or "God's stewardship."

What is most striking, however, is that in three of these passages *oikonomia* is coupled with *mysterion* (mystery). Compare I Cor. 4:1: "This is how one should regard us, as servants of Christ and stewards of the mysteries of God."

"Stewardship of a mystery" is a strange combination of ideas. Paul liked figures of speech and used them freely; he could coin a phrase or mix a metaphor as well as the next man, so he would have been perfectly capable of arriving at this by himself, but it seems likely that the stewardship concept was a legacy from Jesus' teaching, while "mystery" and revelation represented his own experience, and in this phrase he combined the two. Paul wrote, partially quoting Isaiah 64:4, "What no eye has seen, nor ear heard, nor the heart of man conceived, what God has prepared for those who love him, God has revealed to us through the spirit" (I Cor. 2:9,10). This was the mystery of which he felt himself a steward.

But there is also another mystery—a more worldly mystery—to be considered here.

The Steward Vanishes

If before he began his ministry Jesus had been a steward, everybody must soon have known it. In Galilee, where he did much—perhaps most—of his preaching, he was no mysterious stranger. He had grown up there; his family and his disciples were known to each other and to the public; by the end of his life he was, at the very least, a celebrity. His background would have been a matter of common knowledge, and his use of parables drawn from the steward's life would have seemed quite natural to his hearers. How, then, could all knowledge of that life vanish from the record?

That, of course, is part of a larger mystery: how did *all* information about his early manhood vanish completely?

Perhaps this is the origin of that mystery: perhaps with time, and with the growing acceptance of Jesus as the Messiah, the church gradually ceased to discuss what it knew of his early life because his literal stewardship had become an embarrassment.

It meant, for one thing, that all those years he was not a solitary prophet biding his time in self-imposed obscurity; he was out in the world earning his living like everybody else—working and planning, winning and losing, hassled by all the exasperating facts of ordinary life.

It meant, for another thing, that he must have been handling money. I had not realized, until I saw it pointed out in an old book, that in the gospels Jesus is never depicted touching money. His disciples buy food as necessary, Philip or Judas carries the common purse, Peter pays the temple tax. Even when, in answering a question, he illustrates his answer with a coin, Jesus does not pick up the coin himself; he says, “Show me a coin,” and the implication is that the coin is held out before him but he does not touch it (Matt. 22:18,19, Luke 20:24). Whether this represents historical fact or simply reverent reporting, it does probably represent the way many Christians came to feel about Jesus—that he and “Mammon” could have no possible contact with each other. How then could he be presented as a steward?

But the real sticking point, perhaps, was this: if one is a steward one must be a steward *to another person*. Jesus, the Master, must have had an earthly master of his own; must have had to take orders and to say, “Yes, sir,” “No, sir,” and “I’ll see to it today!” To have a boss and to do what he wants, to be praised or blamed accordingly, is part of the “human condition,” at least for working people, and if Jesus was truly man, as the church holds, he accepted all the conditions of man’s life. “He emptied himself,” said Paul, “taking the form of a servant.”

Paul must have known a good deal about Jesus’ career, since he had collected enough evidence against him to persecute his followers, but he says nothing else, in his extant letters, about Jesus’ earthly life and works. Of course those letters must be only a tiny residue of what Paul actually wrote, but they are all we have to go by. We can never know, therefore, the whole significance of his statement to the Corinthians: “I decided to know nothing among you except Jesus Christ, and him crucified” (I Cor. 2:2).

As the gospel began to be preached more and more to Gentiles and to people who had not known Jesus or his immediate disciples, his stewardship might have become an awkwardness, better not mentioned. Besides, it is said, what people wanted to hear were the teachings, the miracles, and most of all, the death and resurrection. There was no need to chronicle the unimportant early years. And so little by little a veil was drawn, it may be, over that part of his life.

How much of this happened of itself as the gospel was spread by word of mouth or in laboriously copied manuscripts it is impossible to tell, but it seems also to have led to an editorial practice of suppressing, even in the parables, any mention of a steward—*oikonomos*—as such. The stories were too important and perhaps already too well-known to be ignored, but care seems to have been taken to avoid the specific word as a possible reminder of Jesus' worldly occupation. Jesus referred to himself as a *diakonos*, and that could be accepted as a graceful figure of speech, but *oikonomos* was apparently taboo.

There is a single reference in Luke (12:42) to a "faithful and wise steward" who looks after the household staff, but in Matthew's version of the same passage he is called simply the "faithful and wise servant," and that is the practice followed most of the time.

The "servants" in The Talents and The Pounds who are expected to trade with their master's money are clearly stewards, or acting as such, and so are the men sent to collect the rent from the Wicked Husbandmen. The Unmerciful Servant who runs up a huge debt to his master while loan-sharking among the lesser servants must have been a steward, and so, in spite of the accepted translation, must the *oikodespotes* who finds himself caught between the jealous Laborers in the Vineyard and the open-handed owner of it.

A striking exception to general practice is the parable of the Unjust (Dishonest) Steward (discussed in the following chapter), which uses *oikonomos* four times; in fact, it is the only parable (except for The Faithful and Wise Steward, mentioned above) which contains the word. What prompted this exception it may be useless to speculate, especially in view of the strange nature of the story itself, which seems to contradict all Jesus' other teachings on loyalty and honesty.

But a comparison of parallel passages in Matthew and Luke best illustrates, in my opinion, the tendency mentioned above to push the steward into the background, or even, as in this case, out of the picture entirely. Matthew 6:24 says:

> No one (*oudeis*) can serve two masters: for either he will hate the one and love the other, or else he will be

> devoted to the one and despise the other. You cannot serve God and Mammon.

Luke 16:13 is identical except for one additional word:

> No servant (*oudeis oiketes*) can serve two masters: for either he will hate the one and love the other, or else he will be devoted to the one and despise the other. You cannot serve God and Mammon.

Matthew's version appears to be complete and in fact has become proverbial ("No man can serve two masters"); why does Luke insert the awkward word *oiketes*: a household servant, a menial or slave? This does not enhance the meaning of the saying; it detracts from it by making it both less general and less appropriate. A menial servant can quite well serve two masters and may be required to do so, and it is not of critical importance whether he loves them or hates them as he fills their baths or cleans their shoes.

I suspect that the original saying was "No steward (*oudeis oikonomos*) can serve two masters." It is the steward whose loyalty is important, for the steward controls his master's property and acts on his behalf; he must not have a conflict of interests. Moreover the saying occurs in the context of several sayings on stewardship (Luke 16: 10-12).

If this suspicion is well-founded it means that editors of the two gospels, acting independently of each other, have each eliminated mention of the steward as such: in Luke by altering the key word (from *oikonomos* to *oiketes*) and in Matthew by simply dropping it.

3

Stewardship as a Recurring Theme

Changing Views

What Jesus actually said, and when and where he said it, are now very hard to determine, but most Biblical scholars agree that the parables are among the most trustworthy of his sayings, the most nearly a true reflection of "the mind that was in Christ Jesus." This is partly because they are so surprising in their setting and application that they are unlikely to have been invented and attributed to him by reverent followers, and partly because they hang together so well as a body of teachings that they do seem to have come from the same mind.

Many of the stories must have come from his own years as a steward, a somewhat unusual background from which to speak to the masses. What is a steward? A poor man, usually, who undertakes to help a rich man get richer, and may be suspected of lining his own pockets in the process: not exactly your popular hero. But Jesus, picturing God as the strict but benevolent master and speaking from his own experience in serving such a man, was able to captivate the common people, who "heard him gladly."

Jesus was an outdoor preacher much of the time, and no doubt the parable was a useful device for engaging the attention of his hearers. This is like the practice of frontier preachers in America, who liked to begin with a story of daily life or adventure, as far removed from the religious mood as possible. The more practical, or humorous, or even grotesque, the better, in order to capture the attention of the crowd, who then had two reasons to listen: first to hear the punch line and second to see how the preacher could possibly turn it to religious advantage.

Most of the stories as they have come down to us are drawn from ordinary life, though some seem to have evolved into more sensational forms. They have been interpreted in differing ways at different times: in the Middle Ages, and in fact from very early times, as allegories; in later centuries as moral teachings for guidance in life—which is the sense in which most of us are familiar with them; and, according to one theory, as "weapons of controversy" used by Jesus against his opponents, and later reworked by the church for its own purposes.

The allegorical method[1] with its often absurd results has long since been abandoned by most interpreters. The "weapons of controversy" theory is hard to accept for many of the parables. It is strange to think that Jesus would take compassion on the crowds because they were "as sheep without a shepherd" (Matt. 9:36), and then, instead of giving them the words of life, harangue them with stories designed to show up his opponents.

A recently popular point of view from which to consider the parables is the study of the social and economic makeup of Galilee in Jesus' time. This has created a school of interpretation very critical of Jesus' words as reported and inclined to question the traditional readings of them. An example is a recent paper on the Parable of the Talents, in which the author wonders how this story would have been understood by a peasant, a poor farmer, in first-century Palestine. If anything like the present version actually goes back to Jesus, says the author, "we are left to wonder how Jesus told a story so obviously given from the vantage point of the elite and so sharply out of touch with the peasant perception of the world."[2] My belief is that Jesus' hearers, including the poor, were quite realistic. They knew that he had spent years as a steward and was using examples frankly from his own experience (something an audience always appreciates) to teach a basic lesson which had many interpretations, on many levels. Perhaps he expounded on the lesson by giving other examples, but perhaps he did not need to. The Gospels record several incidents in which Jesus' teachings are challenged by his hearers, but none in which he is accused of class-consciousness.

This leaves, for the purposes of this book, the conventional view of the parables as designed for general instruction: which, without denying that there may be many subtleties within them, is my point of view.

The heart of the book is the parable of the Talents (the parable of the venture capital), which deals with the responsibility for productivity and "profit," but because so many other parables bear in one way or another on the subject of stewardship and contribute to an understanding of Jesus' outlook, it seems worthwhile to pause here and devote a chapter to a brief review of these other parables.

Housekeeping and Hospitality

The references to housekeeping and hospitality seem perhaps the least significant, but they are interesting as showing Jesus' familiarity with household matters, and hence the likelihood that he was a steward literally and not merely figuratively. Various references to baking, mending, and so forth (sometimes counted as parables, sometimes not) are usually explained as "home memories"—Jesus harking back to his mother's work around the house. It would seem strange, however, that he should make so many references to his mother's work and none to his father's—which was also, according to tradition, his own. It seems more likely that these echoes of household concerns come from his days as a servant and a supervisor of servants.

> The kingdom of heaven is like leaven which a woman took and hid in three measures of flour, till it was all leavened (Matt. 13:33 and similarly Luke 13:21).
>
> You are the salt of the earth; but if salt has lost its taste, how shall its saltness be restored? It is no longer good for anything except to be thrown out and trodden underfoot by men (Matt. 5:13 and similarly Mark 9:50, Luke 14:34).[3]
>
> You are the light of the world. A city set on a hill cannot be hid. Nor do men light a lamp and put it under a bushel, but on a stand, and it gives light to all in the house (Matt. 5:14,15 and similarly Luke 8:16).
>
> No one puts a piece of unshrunk cloth on an old garment, for the patch tears away from the garment, and a worse tear is made. Neither is new wine put into old wineskins; if it is, the skins burst, and the wine is spilled, and the skins are destroyed (Matt. 9:16,17 and similarly Mark 2:21,22, Luke 5:36,37).

Many of the parables naturally deal with servants and service; one is the story called, variously, The Farmer and his Man, The Bondservant, or The Servant's Reward. Here Jesus addresses, presumably, the small landholders:

> Will any one of you, who has a servant plowing or keeping sheep, say to him when he has come in from the field, "Come at once and sit down at table"? Will he not rather say to him, "Prepare supper for me, and gird yourself and serve me, till I eat and drink, and afterward you shall eat and drink"? Does he thank the servant because he did what was commanded? So you also, when you have done all that is commanded you,

> say, "We are unworthy servants; we have only done what was our duty" (Luke 17:7-10).

Two other servant parables are discussed in other chapters but may be listed here: The Servant of Two Masters (Chapter 2) and The Servants Left in Charge (Chapter 4).

Preparations for a feast and for the reception of guests would have been one of the steward's responsibilities, so it is not surprising to find such occasions serving as the basis for many parables: Places at Table, which deals with the seating of guests (Luke 14:7-11); The Friend at Midnight, who borrows bread from a neighbor to feed a late-arriving guest (Luke 11:5-8); The Wise and Foolish Maidens preparing to greet the bridegroom's party as it arrives by lamplight (Matt. 25:1-13); and others.[4]

Five of these stories refer to a marriage feast, and Christian tradition has at times made much of this as a symbol of the union between Christ and his church. But the emphasis in the parables is not on marriage itself; there is no mention of a bride, and a bridegroom appears only once, offstage (in the parable of the Foolish Maidens) and once in another passage when Jesus refers to himself figuratively as the bridegroom, or central figure. In the other cases the fact that they are called wedding feasts seems to be incidental; a wedding feast is the archetypal gala occasion, but it might have been any splendid meal.

The emphasis is not on the food, either. It is on various themes: humility, generosity, response to prayer, reasons for fasting and feasting, readiness for the coming of the Kingdom. The "festive board" was something for which Jesus simply seems to have had a natural affinity, whether as servant, guest, or host, and it served as the setting for many of his tales.

Among the parables of hospitality are two versions of the story of the Unwilling Guests, the point of which is that if those who are invited reject God's invitation, he will fill their places with others. Like several other parables, this has been preserved in two forms.

What sounds like the original story, as told by Jesus (I will call it the "Galilean version") is relatively simple and realistic, a story of ordinary life. But that is not impressive enough for some tastes, and so there develops in the retelling a secondary version, a "Byzantine version," in which everything is bigger, more highly colored, more terrible. The principal character is no longer just a man or even a rich man, but a king; sums of money increase to fabulous proportions; the action is violent and involved, and the end is bloody.

Here is the simpler, or "Galilean" version of The Great Banquet, or The Unwilling Guests, from Luke:

> A man once gave a great banquet, and invited many; and at the time for the banquet he sent his servant to say to those who had been invited, "Come; for all is now ready." But they all alike began to make excuses. The first said to him, "I have bought a field, and I must go out and see it; I pray you, have me excused." And another said, "I have bought five yoke of oxen, and I go to examine them; I pray you, have me excused." And another said, "I have married a wife, and therefore I cannot come." So the servant came, and reported this to his master. Then the householder in anger said to his servant, "Go out quickly to the streets and lanes of the city, and bring in the poor and maimed and blind and lame." And the servant said, "Sir, what you commanded has been done, and still there is room." And the master said to the servant, "Go out to the highways and hedges, and compel people to come in, that my house may be filled. For I tell you, none of those men who were invited shall taste my banquet" (Luke 14:16-24).

Matthew's gospel has the "Byzantine" version, The Marriage Feast. The central figure, described in Luke simply as "a man," is here a king;

the banquet has become a marriage feast for the king's son; the actions are no longer those of a generous but strong-willed man but of a "Byzantine tyrant." When the invited guests snubbed him,

> … the king was angry, and he sent his troops and destroyed those murderers and burned their city. Then he said to his servant, 'The wedding is ready, but those invited were not worthy. Go therefore to the thoroughfares, and invite to the marriage feast as many as you find.' And those servants went out into the streets and gathered all whom they found, both bad and good; so the wedding hall was filled with guests (Matt. 22: 7-10).[5]

Agriculture

The agricultural parables involve another form of stewardship, and lend themselves naturally to Jesus' interest in growth, productivity and abundance. So we have, on the one hand, The Budding Fig Tree (Mark 13:28, Matt. 24:32,33 and similarly Luke 21:29-31), The Seed Growing Secretly (Mark 4:26-29), The Sower's seed that yields a hundredfold (Mark 4:3-8, Matt. 13:3-8), and the tiny Mustard Seed that becomes the greatest of shrubs (Mark 4:30-32, Matt. 13:31, 32, Luke 13:18,19). On the other hand we hear of some of the Sower's seed that falls by the wayside and dies (Mark 4:4), and of a wheat crop threatened by sabotage (The Wheat and the Tares):

> The kingdom of heaven may be compared to a man who sowed good seed in his field, but while men were sleeping, his enemy came and sowed weeds among the wheat, and went away. So when the plants came up and bore grain, then the weeds appeared also. And the servants of the householder came and said to him,

> "Sir, did you not sow good seed in your field? How then has it weeds?" He said to them, "An enemy has done this." The servants said to him, "Then do you want us to go and gather them?" But he said, "No, lest in gathering the weeds you root up the wheat along with them. Let both grow together until the harvest; and at harvest time I will tell the reapers, Gather the weeds first and bind them in bundles to be burned, but gather the wheat into my barn" (Matt. 13:24-30).

Another story of judgement deferred is called The Barren Fig Tree:

> A man had a fig tree planted in his vineyard; and he came seeking fruit on it and found none. And he said to the vinedresser, "Lo, these three years I have come seeking fruit on this fig tree, and I find none. Cut it down; why should it use up the ground?" And he answered him, "Let it alone, sir, this year also, till I dig about it and put on manure. And if it bears fruit next year, well and good; but if not, you can cut it down" (Luke 13:6-9).

This parable is unusual in that it pictures the employee as pleading for the tree and winning the owner over to his point of view. We might have expected to hear the practical vinedresser argue for cutting it down and the patient owner saying, as in the Wheat and the Tares, "Don't be hasty: let's give it more time." One theory holds that the parable has been altered in order to symbolize Christ pleading for mankind.

The image of the harvest appears in all the gospels:

> The kingdom of God is as if a man should scatter seed upon the ground and should sleep and rise night

> and day, and the seed should sprout and grow, he knows not how. The earth produces of itself, first the blade, then the ear, then the full grain in the ear. But when the grain is ripe, at once he puts in the sickle, because the harvest time has come (Mark 4:26-29).

> Lift up your eyes, and see how the fields are already white for harvest (John 4:35).

> The harvest is plentiful, but the laborers are few; pray therefore the Lord of the harvest to send out laborers into his harvest (Matt. 9:37,38, Luke 10:2).

There are not as many agricultural parables as one might expect, given the time and place in which they were told, but because the rustic scene is naturally attractive and because Jesus was often in such a scene, he is frequently thought of as a kind of nature poet. A passage from Renan's *Life of Jesus* is an example:

> His [early] preaching was gentle and pleasing, breathing Nature and the perfume of the fields. He loved the flowers, and took from them his most charming lessons. The birds of heaven, the sea, the mountains, and the games of children furnished in turn the subject of his instructions.[6]

S. Parks Cadman's *Parables of Jesus* says:

> Not a few of his stories are aromatic with the dewy scents of his home in the Galilean hills. They visualize a fair, sweet, joyous landscape: the music of its birds, the green of its trees, the sound of its rippling waters; a landscape crowded with beautiful sceneries, and the breath of flowers, the golden waves of harvest, the gleam of stars on moving seas.[7]

Such passages could be collected by the hundreds. This is Jesus as we like to think of him: the gentle prophet roaming the fields on appleblossom feet and drawing his inspiration from all the scenes around him; but actually, birds and flowers, seas and mountains play a very small part in his teachings. Even his rustic parables are more likely to be of people than of natural processes alone, and there are not many altogether. No doubt some have been lost.

A slender volume called *Beyond the Gospels*, by Roderic Dunkerley, contains a collection of reported sayings of Jesus which have come down to us from sources outside the accepted Gospels.[8] Many of them appear to be simply paraphrases of well-known sayings from the Gospels and others are in a quite different language and deliberately enigmatic, but some jibe very well with the picture of the agricultural steward. From this book I give three extracts.

The first is from the Blickling Homilies, written in Anglo-Saxon, probably about the time of King Alfred:

> We know that Christ himself said by his own mouth, When ye see growing and blowing all the fruits of the earth, and the fragrant odours exhaling from plants, then soon afterwards they shall dry up and dwindle away on account of the summer's heat.[9]

The brief life of the grass and flowers is a common idea in the Old Testament and hardly original with Jesus, but this is an unusually vivid passage; it is an appealing glimpse of him delighting in a summer's day, yet the actual message is the shortness of life. "We must work the works of him who sent me, while it is day. Night comes, when no one can work" (John 9:4).

Another passage, says Dunkerley, comes from "a strange medieval Moslem romance entitled *The Gospel of Barnabas*… [which] retells the Gospel story in the interests of Islam, Jesus being made to predict the coming of Mohammed, and so forth." It may have been based on an early apocryphal book of the same name. In it is the following parable, attributed to Jesus:

> There was a man who had great possessions, and in his territory he had desert land that only bore unfruitful things. And so, as he was walking one day through such desert land he found among such unfruitful plants a plant that had delicate fruits. Whereupon he said, Now how doth this plant here bear these so delicate fruits? Assuredly I will not that it be cut down and put on the fire with the rest. And having called his servants, he made them dig it up and set it in his garden. Even so I tell you that our God shall reserve from the flames of hell those who work righteousness, wheresoever they be.[10]

Dunkerley comments that this reminds us of Acts 10:35: "In every nation he that feareth him and worketh righteousness is accepted with him," but he feels that the chances of its coming from Jesus himself is remote.

My feeling is just the opposite. The emphasis on fruitfulness is pure Jesus, and so is the whole structure of the story: the restless rich man reviewing his land inch by inch, the sharp eye that spies the one fruitful plant, the quick command to the servants to save it. It recalls Jesus' saying in the incident of the Roman centurion: "I tell you, many will come from east and west and sit at table with Abraham, Isaac and Jacob in the kingdom of heaven" (Matt. 8:11).

A third story from the same collection was ascribed to Jesus by Papias and quoted by Irenaeus in the second century; it runs as follows:

> The days will come in which vines shall grow, each having ten thousand shoots, and on one shoot ten thousand branches, and on one branch again ten

> thousand twigs, and on each twig ten thousand clusters, and in each cluster ten thousand grapes, and each grape when pressed shall yield five-and-twenty measures of wine. And when any of the saints shall have taken hold of one of the clusters another shall cry, I am a better cluster, take me, bless the Lord through me. Likewise also a grain of wheat shall produce ten thousand heads, and every head shall have ten thousand grains, and every grain ten pounds of fine flour, bright and clean; and the other fruits, seeds, and the grass shall produce in similar proportions; and all the animals, using these fruits which are products of the soil, shall become in their turn peaceable and harmonious, obedient to man in all subjection.[11]

This rococo composition does not seem at all like Jesus, at least at first sight, yet if you read it again you see—though here fantastically expanded and embellished—the familiar emphasis on growth and abundance.

Debtors and Creditors

Now, in sharp contrast to the "nature poet" image of Jesus, consider this passage from the work of German historian Adolf Hausrath:

> The most frequent images in the utterances of Jesus are those of the creditor, the debtor, and the debtors' prison. In one parable, everybody except the king is bankrupt; the steward is in debt to the king, the servants to the steward (Matt. 18:23); the rich who remit to their debtors fifty or five hundred pence are rare indeed (Luke 6:34, 7:41,42); the unmerciful creditor who always has the bailiff at hand is much

> more frequent. In the street, the creditor seizes the poor debtor, and the judge's officer casts him into prison, out of which he does not depart until he has paid the very last farthing (Luke 12:58,59); and if he cannot pay, his lord commands him to be sold, and his wife and children, and all that he has, and payment to be made (Matt. 18:25). Oil and wheat, the first necessaries of life, are furnished on credit (Luke 16:5-7); buildings that have been commenced remain unfinished for want of money (Luke 14:28, 29); the merchant puts all his means, in order to keep them safe, into a single pearl (Matt. 13:45,46); in digging in the field, one finds the treasure which another has buried to keep it from the rapacious hands of the oppressor (Matt. 13:44) [and so on].[12]

Hausrath simply wanted to bring out the hard economic times in which Jesus lived, and this picture is as much exaggerated in its way as the poetic one, but it does act as an antidote to an oversentimentalized view.

Jesus did not dwell quite so heavily on the subject of debt as claimed by Hausrath, but, as has been mentioned, he did speak often of money and wealth in general. This is considered a paradox. Was it not he who said, "It is easier for a camel to go through the eye of a needle than for a rich man to enter the kingdom of God" and "You cannot serve God and mammon"? Yet in one parable after another, wealth and the making of wealth are presented as something to be desired, and the rich man as occupying a position crudely analogous to that of God. Obviously the wealth Jesus speaks of is symbolic, but why did he make so much use of this paradoxical theme?

I believe, as I have already stated, that it was because it was near at hand, coming directly out of his personal and recent experiences. The facts that money is of interest to everyone, in some degree, and that money transactions are more easily understood than philosophical abstractions would also be reasons to use them, though no doubt Jesus could have found other symbols as useful—and perhaps less confusing.

Preachers and writers sometimes speak of Jesus' "teachings on money," but Jesus taught very little about actual money. "Do not lay up for yourselves treasures on earth" (Matt. 6:19-21) and "Render to Caesar the things that are Caesar's" (Mark 12:17, Luke 20:25) about cover it. Unless we accept the words "Make friends for yourselves by means of unrighteous mammon" as authentic words of Jesus, all the rest are parabolic teachings in which wealth stands for spiritual good of various kinds.

It probably makes little difference in what order one considers these parables, but since we have begun with the subject of debtors and creditors we may as well plunge into the ones that deal with that. The most elaborate is The Unmerciful Servant (The Grasping Steward). It is usually assumed that this "servant" was a steward who had used his position of trust to amass a fortune at his master's expense. It is found only in Matthew and has the features typical of what I have called a "Byzantine" version. The central figure is a king, the major debt is enormous (ten thousand talents represents millions of dollars), the action is violent and the end is cruel.

> The kingdom of heaven may be compared to a king who wished to settle accounts with his servants. When he began the reckoning, one was brought to him who owed him ten thousand talents; and as he could not pay, his lord ordered him to be sold, with his wife and children and all that he had, and payment to be made. So the servant fell on his knees, imploring him, "Lord, have patience with me, and I will pay you everything." And out of pity for him the lord of that servant released him and forgave him the debt. But that same servant, as he went out, came

> upon one of his fellow servants who owed him a hundred denarii. And seizing him by the throat he said, "Pay what you owe." So his fellow servant fell down and besought him, "Have patience with me, and I will pay you." He refused and went and put him in prison till he should pay the debt. When his fellow servants saw what had taken place, they were greatly distressed, and they went and reported to their lord all that had taken place. Then his lord summoned him and said to him, "You wicked servant! I forgave you all that debt because you besought me; and should you not have had mercy on your fellow servant, as I had mercy on you?" And in anger his lord delivered him to the jailers till he should pay all his debt. So also my heavenly Father will do to every one of you, if you do not forgive your brother from your heart (Matt. 18:23-35).

I cannot help seeing behind this story a simpler, "Galilean" version: not only because the present story has all the earmarks of a secondary version but also because the plot is not intrinsically regal. If the commander of the king's army had raised a rebellion against him and the king had pardoned him, only to find the same commander brutally punishing one of his own men for some small offense—such a story might require, or at least justify, a king as protagonist. But this is a simple matter of debtors and creditors.

In this (probably rather commonplace) story of corruption, the conviction and punishment of the steward are expected by the hearers, and relished. Serves him right! The master's forgiveness is not expected, but must be accepted, since the master is notoriously lenient. But then there is a new development, which seems at first like an anti-climax but turns out to be the true climax, to which the rest of the story leads up. The forgiven steward is found abusing one of his own debtors, and the hitherto kind and generous master speaks out in wrath against him and this time does punish him, not for his crime but for his heartlessness toward his fellow servant.

Forgiveness is also the theme of The Two Debtors (The Great and Little Debtors):

> A certain creditor had two debtors; one owed five hundred denarii, and the other fifty. When they could not pay, he forgave them both. Now which of them will love him more?" Simon answered, "The one, I suppose, to whom he forgave more." And he said to him, "You have judged rightly" (Luke 7:41-43).

Another brief story is called The Defendant, or Going Before the Judge, or Settling Out of Court:

> Why do you not judge for yourselves what is right? As you go with your accuser before the magistrate, make an effort to settle with him on the way, lest he drag you to the judge, and the judge hand you over to the officer, and the officer put you in prison. I tell you, you will never get out till you have paid the very last copper (Luke 12:57-59 and similarly Matt. 5:25,26).

There is still another parable that involves debt, but in which the ending is so baffling that there is no agreement as to the "moral" of the story. This is The Unjust Steward (The Dishonest Steward):

> There was a rich man who had a steward, and charges were brought to him that this man was wasting his goods. And he called him and said to him, "What is this I hear about you? Turn in the account of your stewardship, for you can no longer be steward." And

> the steward said to himself, "What shall I do, since my master is taking the stewardship away from me? I am not strong enough to dig, and I am ashamed to beg. I have decided what to do, so that people may receive me into their houses when I am put out of the stewardship." So, summoning his master's debtors one by one, he said to the first, "How much do you owe my master?" He said, "A hundred measures of oil." And he said to him, "Take your bill and sit down quickly and write fifty." Then he said to another, "And how much do you owe?" He said, "A hundred measures of wheat." He said to him, "Take your bill and write eighty." The master commended the dishonest steward for his prudence; for the sons of this world are wiser in their own generation than the sons of light. And I tell you, make friends for yourselves by means of unrighteous mammon, so that when it fails they may receive you into the eternal habitations (Luke 16:1-9).

Many churchgoing Christians are unfamiliar with this parable and when they chance to read it refuse to believe their eyes. If they retire to the library and look up interpretations they can find plenty of them; someone has counted 36 schools of thought on the subject. I have seen only a few of these, but none is convincing to me, and obviously none of the 36 authors is convinced by the reasoning of the others. Many have tried to justify the steward on the grounds, for instance, that he was befriending the poor by reducing their indebtedness to his hard-hearted master, or that he was reducing it by the amount of his own commission, and so forth, but as has been said, "All attempts to white-wash the steward have failed." Some commentators have suggested that the whole thing was heavy irony on Jesus' part, or badly translated, or not one of Jesus' parables at all.

The puzzle is all the more puzzling when the parable is read—as it usually is—together with the verses immediately following:

> He who is faithful in a very little is faithful also in much; and he who is dishonest in a very little is dishonest also in much. If then you have not been faithful in the unrighteous mammon, who will entrust to you the true riches? And if you have not been faithful in that which is another's, who will give you that which is your own? No servant can serve two masters; for either he will hate the one and love the other, or he will be devoted to the one and despise the other. You cannot serve God and mammon (Luke 16:10-13).

The discussion becomes very complicated, but the short note by J. B. Phillips, author of *The Gospels Translated into Modern English*, covers the main points:

> This story recorded by St. Luke is well known for its difficulty of interpretation. Most commentators suggest that the lesson to be learned is that the follower of Christ should be as shrewd about his spiritual future as the rascally steward was about his own immediate security. Personally, I do not feel satisfied with this view as it introduces a note of careful calculation which is quite at variance with Christ's teaching elsewhere. Moreover, the passage in question goes on to state categorically that dishonesty in earthly things is bound to mean dishonesty in the greater, or spiritual things, and this seems a very odd conclusion to be drawn from this parable![13]

My own feeling is that no interpretation is possible, because what is under consideration is not one parable but parts of two, patched together, as a consequence of a lost page or some other damage to the text.

As the story begins it is told in direct dialogue and the plot is hard-edged and crystal clear, through the words, "Take your bill and write eighty." It would play on stage or screen today. Scene One, Front Office: Owner and Steward. Scene Two, Steward's Office: Steward and Debtors. Curtain rises on Steward soliloquizing about his plight. Enter First Debtor; etc. There is a brisk dialogue as the steward hastily contrives to cook the books before his departure. Scene Three ought to be the climax, the big confrontation scene in which the steward's cleverness is revealed and the boss's judgement, for or against him, is pronounced in memorable words.

But, surprise! There is no Scene Three. Instead the action is suddenly terminated by an offstage voice, saying, "The master commended the dishonest steward for his prudence, for the sons of this world are wiser in their own generation than the children of light." What happened to Scene Three? Whenever one of the parables is presented in this dramatic form, with the characters speaking their lines directly, it usually ends with a ringing pronouncement by the master of the situation. Why, in this case, is there such a feeble and unconvincing climax?

I think it is because the ending comes from another story, told in a different style. Both Matthew and Mark state that Jesus "said nothing to them [the crowds] without a parable," so there must originally have been many more parables than those which have come down to us; and since stewardship was one of Jesus' favorite themes, many of those lost stories doubtless dealt with that. In this passage Luke gives one which none of the other gospels has, along with several other stewardship sayings (verses 10 to 13) also unique to this gospel. He apparently had a special source which included a collection of such parables and sayings, and it may be that a page or some part of one, containing the true ending of our story, was lost, and the next surviving page or fragment included the end of *another* stewardship story, one about an *honest* steward.

Suppose, for instance, that this other story, the gist of which we don't know, concluded, "The master commended the honest (*dikaios*) steward," a statement that would lead easily into the passage on faithfulness (verses 10-13). But a copyist who was unaware that a part of the text was missing and who was simply following the original story line might decide that the text was faulty (the steward was flagrantly dishonest!): and might "correct" it by changing *dikaios* to *adikias* (dishonest), thus creating a dishonest steward, and riveting this conclusion to the parable for all time. With the addition of some editorial interpretation, including the mention of "prudence," that is the parable as we have it now.

It is true that there seems to be no alternative version of the text, no evidence that it ever read differently. It is said that Julian the Apostate, the Roman emperor who was brought up as a Christian but converted to paganism, cited this parable as one of the factors in his disillusionment, so he must have had essentially the same version we have. But this may simply mean that the damage occurred early in the history of the text.

Everyone agrees that there seems to be something terribly wrong with the story. It "does not compute." The idea that the master who dismissed the servant for "wasting his goods" would turn right around and praise him for fraud is hard to accept. Some interpreters argue that the "lord" (*kyrios*) who commended the dishonest steward was not the master in the parable but Jesus himself, in a paradoxical mood, but that is even harder to accept. Jesus constantly preached faithfulness to trust. "Who will be that faithful and wise steward?" "Well done, thou good and faithful servant." This very passage from Luke contains three more sayings on faithful stewardship.

The conventional explanations do not compute, either; the strained explanation that "the followers of Christ should be as shrewd as the rascally steward was about his own immediate security" is really useless because it is impossible to find any analogy in the story beyond those words, unless it implies that one should make a few deals with the devil so that when God rejects him he can hope for a comfortable room in hell!

A final objection is that this story, if correct as it stands, would be that it is the only one of Jesus' parables in which the lesson was the actual use of worldly goods; in all others the wealth of this world is a symbol for something else. Even if one discounts the injunction "Make friends for yourselves by means of unrighteous mammon" as an editorial addition, that does seem to be the only logical advice to be drawn from the story; and this literal treatment of money is so uncharacteristic of Jesus that it cries out for attention, like a wrong technique in a forged painting.

We can't ignore the text we are given, but where difficulties pile up to this extent we should at least consider the possibility that the text is faulty, and beware of any conclusions based on it.

Trouble with Tenants

The story of The Wicked Husbandmen (The Cruel Vinedressers, The Rebellious Tenant Farmers) is another of the "Byzantine" tales. In this case all the synoptic gospels give essentially the same story, the most elaborate version being that found in Matthew, where Jesus says:

> "There was a householder who planted a vineyard, and set a hedge around it, and dug a wine press in it, and built a tower[14], and let it out to tenants, and went into another country. When the season of fruit drew near, he sent his servants to the tenants, to get his fruit; and the tenants took his servants and beat one, killed another, and stoned another. Again he sent other servants, more than the first; and they did

> the same to them. Afterward he sent his son to them, saying, 'They will respect my son.' But when the tenants saw the son, they said to themselves, 'This is the heir; come, let us kill him and have his inheritance.' And they took him and cast him out of the vineyard, and killed him. When therefore the owner of the vineyard comes, what will he do with those tenants?" They said to him, "He will put those wretches to a miserable death, and let out the vineyard to other tenants who will give him the fruits in their seasons" (Matt. 21:33-41 and similarly Mark 12:1-9, Luke 20:9-16).

A different kind of problem comes up in The Empty House (The Return of the Unclean Spirit):

> When the unclean spirit has gone out of a man, he [the spirit] passes through waterless places seeking rest; and finding none, he says, I will return to my house from which I came. And when he comes he finds it swept and put in order. Then he goes and brings seven other spirits more evil than himself, and they enter and dwell there; and the last state of that man becomes worse than the first (Matt. 12:43-45, Luke 11:24-26).

This story, as usually interpreted, is one of the simplest and clearest of the parables. It warns that repentance is not enough; the evil that has been driven out of a soul—the sin or madness—must be replaced by active habits of love and righteousness or the evil will creep back, bringing others with it.

The gospel text looks like a mixture, such as might be remembered by a hearer in later years, of the parable itself and the interpretation of it. One could easily reconstruct such a parable. It would be familiar to many a modern landlord; call it "The Squatters." He, the landlord, has an undesirable tenant who is ruining his house, so he evicts him and cleans and redecorates the house in preparation for renting it again. But there is a delay in getting a new tenant in, and the house stands empty for a time. Meanwhile the former tenant returns, sizes up the situation and sneaks back in, bringing seven friends with him, and the last state of that house is worse than the first. The customary interpretation applies perfectly.

That this analogy suggested itself to Jesus because of his experience as a steward seems extremely likely.

A Wage Dispute, and Other Economic Themes

A question of equity is at the bottom of the parable called The Laborers in the Vineyard (The Laborers and the Hours, The Good Employer):

> The kingdom of heaven is like a householder who went out early in the morning to hire laborers for his vineyard. After agreeing with the laborers for a denarius a day, he sent them into his vineyard. And going out about the third hour he saw others standing idle in the marketplace; and to them he said, "You go into the vineyard, too, and whatever is right I will give you." So they went. Going out again about the sixth hour and the ninth hour, he did the same. And about the eleventh hour he went out and found others standing; and he said to them, "Why do you stand here idle all day?" They said to him, "Because no one has hired us." He said to them, "You go into the vineyard too." And when evening came, the owner of the vineyard said to his steward, "Call the laborers and pay them their wages, beginning with the last, up to

> the first." And when those hired about the eleventh hour came, each of them received a denarius. Now when the first came, they thought they would receive more; but each of them also received a denarius. And on receiving it they grumbled at the householder, saying, "These last worked only one hour, and you have made them equal to us who have borne the burden of the day and the scorching heat." But he replied to one of them, "Friend, I am doing you no wrong; did you not agree with me for a denarius? Take what belongs to you, and go; I choose to give to this last as I give to you. Am I not allowed to do what I choose with what belongs to me? Or do you begrudge my generosity?" (Matt. 20:1-15)[15]

This parable is often interpreted as referring to late conversions or "late callings," that is, late-life recruits to the ministry or other religious work, or even the late calling of the Gentiles to the Kingdom. In this view the men in the marketplace are deliberately idle. They are just standing around killing time, says this school, and their statement that no one has hired them is a lame excuse by lazy men. The point of the parable is presumed to be the "good employer's" generosity in overlooking long indifference. When the idlers shape up and join the workers, all is forgiven and they are paid as much for the day as the others.

A dissenting opinion holds that they are not idlers; they had waited in the market place all day in hope of employment, and immediately accepted it when offered. This readiness was in itself a form of service, since it made them instantly available when needed, and the employer tacitly acknowledged that by paying them for the full day. In Milton's words, "They also serve who only stand and wait."

Other stewardly sayings involve the care of possessions.

> Do not lay up for yourselves treasures on earth, where moth and rust consume and where thieves break in and steal, but lay up for yourselves treasures in heaven… for where your treasure is, there will your heart be also (Matt. 6:19-21).

> Every scribe who has been trained for the kingdom of heaven is like a householder who brings out of his treasure what is new and what is old (Matt. 13:52).

> How can one enter a strong man's house and plunder his goods, unless he first binds the strong man; then indeed he may plunder his house (Matt. 12:29).

> If the householder had known in what part of the night the thief was coming, he would have watched and would not have let his house be broken into (Matt. 24:43, Luke 12:39).

The references to the "strong man" and "the householder" are obscure. Jesus may have been referring to recent events.

Two parables often linked are The Tower Builder and The King Going to War, though the second account is far removed from Jesus' usual themes.

> Which of you, intending to build a tower, does not first sit down and count the cost, whether he has enough to complete it? Otherwise, when he has laid a foundation and is not able to finish, all who see it begin to mock him, saying, "This man began to build, and was not able to finish."

> Or what king, going to encounter another king in war, will not sit down first and take counsel whether

> he is able with ten thousand to meet him who comes against him with twenty thousand? And if not, while the other is yet a great way off, he sends an embassy and asks terms of peace.
>
> So therefore, whoever of you does not renounce all that he has cannot be my disciple (Luke 14:28-33).

These two are sometimes preached together under the title "Counting the Cost." The would-be follower of Jesus must be prepared to see it through at all cost, or he had better not undertake it at all. A similar warning is found in Luke 9:62: "No one who puts his hand to the plow and looks back is fit for the kingdom of God."

The story of The Prodigal Son is not usually included among the stewardship parables; it is thought of primarily as a tale of fatherly love and forgiveness. But the relationship among the family members is also expressed in terms of their relationship to the family property, of which the elder brother is a faithful, if not always wise, steward.

The first part of the story is known to everybody, more or less: how the younger of two brothers asked his father for his share of the property and went away and squandered it and then, penniless and starving, returned to ask for a job as a hired man on his father's estate. But "while he was yet at a distance, his father saw him and had compassion and ran and embraced him," dressed him in fine clothes and called the neighbors in and made a feast (Luke 15: 11-24). Not everyone everyone remembers so well what happened next:

> Now his elder son was in the field; and as he came and drew near to the house, he heard music and dancing. And he called one of the servants and asked what this meant. And he said to him, "Your brother has come, and your father has killed the fatted calf, because he has received him safe and sound." But he

> was angry and refused to go in. His father came out and entreated him, but he answered his father, "Lo, these many years I have served you, and I never disobeyed your command; yet you never gave me [so much as] a kid, that I might make merry with my friends. But when this son of yours came, who has devoured your living with harlots, you killed for him the fatted calf!" And he said to him, "Son, you are always with me, and all that is mine is yours. It was fitting to make merry and be glad, for this your brother was dead, and is alive; he was lost, and is found" (Luke 15: 25-32).

Some commentators have felt that this part of the story is an anticlimax, and some have even suggested that it is not authentic. When it is discussed, it is usually to pour contempt upon the elder brother. Preachers pull out all the stops when they come to him; he is "heartless," "selfrighteous," "jealous," "churlish," etc. In a Bible study class I once attended, everyone was asked which of the brothers he identified with. It was striking that all those who identified with the prodigal son looked cheerful, not to say smug, while those who identified with the dutiful elder brother looked downcast and ashamed. This is the result of centuries of Christian preaching, but is it the result that Christ intended?

I don't believe that Jesus, who laid so much stress on faithful stewardship, would have slighted the faithful son over a moment's outburst. I believe that the father in the original parable had more words of praise and comfort for him than are recorded here and that the story was told as much for the sake of the stay-at-home as for the prodigal, and with just as much loving concern.

Two other stories from Luke deal with rich men and their property. One is that of The Foolish Rich Man who says, "Soul, you have ample goods laid up for many years; eat, drink, and be merry," only to have God say to him, "Fool! This night your soul is required of you; and the things you have prepared, whose will they be?" Such a fool is he, the story concludes, who lays up treasure for himself, and is not rich toward God (Luke 12:16-21).

The other is that in which a rich man, traditionally called Dives, ignores the needs of the beggar Lazarus at his gate, only to repent when, having died and gone to Hell, he sees "Abraham afar off and Lazarus in his bosom," and begs that Lazarus shall go back to earth and warn Dives' brothers, lest they meet the same fate (Luke 16:19-31).

These stories differ noticeably from those described earlier, in the character of the man on whom they are centered. Most of the parables depict the master, presumably a rich man, as a strict but generous personage. His own life and wealth, his own character and habits are not under judgement; he himself represents judgement. But in these two stories the rich man is the loser, through his own faults.

It seems likely that these last two stories were popular or proverbial tales that, in the years before the Gospels were written down, came to be attributed to Jesus simply because they were moral tales about rich men. Perhaps I am influenced by the desire to make a neat case— to throw out everything that does not fit into my scheme. But even if one accepts them as being truly of Jesus' authorship, they have little bearing on stewardship as I am considering it here, and I have not tried to draw any conclusions from them.

4
Talents and Pounds

I have presented the foregoing summary of parables to demonstrate how much importance Jesus attached to stewardship, but the rest of the book will be devoted to the parable of the Talents and its supposed counterpart, the parable of the Pounds—which is also called the parable of the Prince Royal, or the Claimant to the Throne.

The text of The Talents (in both the King James Version and the Revised Standard Versions of the Bible) has already been given in Chapter I. The text of The Pounds (also in both versions) appears below.

The Parable of the Pounds
(King James Version)

> A certain nobleman went into a far country to receive for himself a kingdom, and to return. And he called his ten servants, and delivered them ten pounds, and said unto them, Occupy till I come.
>
> But his citizens hated him, and sent a message after him, saying, We will not have this man to reign over us.
>
> And it came to pass, that when he was returned, having received the kingdom, then he commanded these servants to be called unto him, to whom he had given

the money, that he might know how much every man had gained by trading.

Then came the first, saying, Lord, thy pound hath gained ten pounds. And he said unto him, Well, thou good servant: because thou hast been faithful in a very little, have thou authority over ten cities. And the second came, saying, Lord, thy pound hath gained five pounds. And he said likewise to him, Be thou also over five cities.

And another came, saying, Lord, behold, here is thy pound, which I have kept laid up in a napkin:

For I feared thee, because thou art an austere man; thou takest up that thou layedst not down, and reapest that thou didst not sow.

And he said unto him, Out of thine own mouth will I judge thee, thou wicked servant. Thou knewest that I was an austere man, taking up that I laid not down, and reaping that I did not sow: Wherefore then gavest not thou my money into the bank, that at my coming I might have required mine own with usury?

And he said unto them that stood by, Take from him the pound, and give it to him that hath ten pounds. (And they said unto him, Lord, he hath ten pounds.)

For I say unto you, That unto every one which hath shall be given; and from him that hath not, even that he hath shall be taken away from him.

But those mine enemies, which would not that I should reign over them, bring hither, and slay them before me (Luke 19:12-27).

Some notes on the text:

He called his ten servants: at the reckoning, only three are mentioned, and the third is referred to in the Greek text as "the other," so three was probably the original number. *Occupy till I come:* the old meaning of "occupy" in English was "to use in commerce," "to trade with." Modern translations give, "Trade with these until I come." *Napkin: soudarion,* a large square of cloth used, like a bandana, for a head-covering or to wipe away sweat.

The Parable of the Pounds (Revised Standard Version)

> A nobleman went into a far country to receive a kingdom and then return. Calling ten of his servants, he gave them ten pounds, and said to them, "Trade with these till I come."
>
> But his citizens hated him and sent an embassy after him, saying, "We do not want this man to reign over us."
>
> When he returned, having received the kingly power, he commanded these servants, to whom he had given the money, to be called to him, that he might know what they had gained by trading.
>
> The first came before him, saying, "Lord, your pound has made ten pounds more." And he said to him, "Well done, good servant! Because you have been faithful in a very little, you shall have authority over ten cities."
>
> And the second came, saying, "Lord, your pound has made five pounds." And he said to him, "And you are to be over five cities."

> Then another came, saying, "Lord, here is your pound, which I kept laid away in a napkin; for I was afraid of you, because you are a severe man; you take up what you did not lay down, and reap what you did not sow."
>
> He said to him, "I will condemn you out of your own mouth, you wicked servant! You knew that I was a severe man, taking up what I did not lay down and reaping what I did not sow? Why then did you not put my money into the bank, and at my coming I should have collected it with interest?" And he said to those who stood by, "Take the pound from him, and give it to him who has the ten pounds."
>
> (And they said to him, "Lord, he has ten pounds!")
>
> "I tell you, that to every one who has will more be given; but from him who has not, even what he has will be taken away.
>
> But as for these enemies of mine, who did not want me to reign over them, bring them here and slay them before me." (Luke 19:12-27)

This is a strange story, with a dreadful ending, and relatively unfamiliar today. Mention the "buried talent" in any company and you will be understood; mention the "hidden pound" and the reaction is probably blank looks. When the parable is preached or discussed at all it is usually only as a companion piece to The Talents, and the gruesome climax is ignored or quickly skipped over. It has seldom, it seems safe to say, been on the list of "best-loved" Bible passages, but in the past it was dutifully read and preached, all the same. If there is judgement, as Christians believe, that includes punishment, in some form. Nevertheless, the customary identification of the "nobleman" with

Jesus presents him in the last scene as not only judging but reveling in slaughter; a picture totally at odds with his known character and teachings, and highly repugnant to most believers.

At first glance the tale appears to be an almost perfect example of what I have called a "Byzantine" parable: the central figure is a king, the plot is complex, and the end is bloody. But this is more than a dressing up of a simpler original; a whole new story has been superimposed on it. It seems to be based on the historical case of Archelaus, the son of Herod the Great, who after his father's death journeyed to Rome to be declared king of Judea and Samaria. His father had bequeathed him the title, but it had to be confirmed by Rome. The Jews, his future subjects, sent a delegation to Rome to try to head off his confirmation, but were unsuccessful. It is hard to understand how this record of a wicked and ultimately disgraced ruler (Archelaus was removed by the Romans ten years later) could have been used as a symbol of divine justice, but it has traditionally been so used.

Thus Jesus is seen as the nobleman, Heaven is the far country, and the Jews or other "unbelievers" are the people who do not want him as their king.

It is often assumed that the main point, in both Talents and Pounds, is the condemnation of the servant who made no effort, but we have this impression only because The Talents is so much better known. Actually The Pounds, as it stands in the Gospel of Luke, teaches two lessons: one of them echoes The Talents, up to a point, while the other introduces a completely different standard. This is possible because it contains two distinct plots and two sets of characters, the only unifying feature being the departure and return of a powerful personage.

On one side of the stage, in this drama, the "servants" take their individual ways with the entrusted money and are rewarded or punished in accordance with their actions; on the other side the rebellious "citizens" are slaughtered not for their deeds, or lack of them, but solely for not wishing to accept the king.

One Story or Two?

Many students of this parable believe that the story of the claimant to the throne was not originally a part of the parable, does not fit convincingly into it, and can, in fact, be lifted out with little damage to the plot of the "traders." For a nobleman in line for a crown to interest himself in a small-time trading venture and follow it up so carefully doesn't ring true, nor does the award of the "loser's" pound to a man who had just been given authority over ten cities. Was this a part of the story as Jesus told it, or was it inserted after his time, for its allegorical significance?

It goes without saying that the traditional version has always been staunchly defended. Richard Chenevix Trench, for example, while admitting the difficulties, argued that if only we keep in mind that "there were two groups of hearers [the disciples and the 'multitude'] in different states of mind and needing different admonitions, to whom the Lord addressed the parable, it will be at once perceived how he divided to all, to his own disciples and to the multitude, according to their different needs."[1]

Alexander Balmain Bruce followed much the same reasoning. He first alludes to a familiar hypothesis that the parable in its present form consists of "two parables originally distinct blended into one—a lost parable concerning a king and his subjects, and Matthew's parable of the talents transformed."

> It cannot be denied that the hypothesis possesses considerable plausibility. For the parable as given by Luke combines traits so diverse, that on first thought one is tempted to regard them as incompatible. The main actor appears to be at once a king and a private person, a nobleman and a tradesman; the persons to whom he is related are partly subjects and partly servants; the sum he gives the latter seems unworthy of

> a king, and the reward he bestows on them, while such as becomes a king, seems inappropriate to the character they have hitherto sustained, which is that of traders. Yet we venture to think that, if only the situation be kept steadily in view, the objections which appear at first so formidable, may to a large extent be removed.[2]

This view is still upheld, and the nobleman still has his supporters. "It is a real misfortune," wrote the Canon of St. Paul's, in 1926, "that those insignificant pounds should have given their name to this great parable, to the almost entire neglect of that more tremendous side of it, which has no place in the title at all and has come to be regarded almost as a clumsy interpolation."[3]

A 1982 article by Luke Timothy Johnson deals almost entirely with the kingship theme. It holds that contrary to conventional opinion, the parable *confirms* the expectation of Luke 19:11, that is, that the kingdom of God would appear immediately: "Jesus *is* proclaimed as a King and does exercise rule through his apostles in the restored Israel. This is a 'manifestation' of God's Kingdom. And those who refuse it, are cut off." In Johnson's interpretation the story of the trading servants gets only a few lines:

> The business of the pounds and servants points to a secondary teaching, the need to deal with material possessions creatively and responsibly in the interim between ascension and *parousia*[4]... [The] political reward for the faithful use of possessions integrates the two parts of the story, and indicates as well that the "political" aspect of the parable [i.e. the story of the nobleman] is not secondary but, in its present version, primary.[5]

To me the impression is inescapable that the story of the vengeful king who slaughters the rebellious subjects, in this parable, is exactly parallel to that of the vengeful host who slaughters the recalcitrant guests, in the parable of the Marriage Feast, and that both these gory episodes, so foreign to the basic stories, were inserted into the parables by overzealous narrators. The early Christians, spurned by the Jews and persecuted by the Romans, must sometimes—however unchristianly—have dreamed of a settling of scores, and these scenes of retribution were someone's expression of that feeling, in just the same way that the Jews had earlier envisioned the destruction of *their* enemies: "Whoever is found will be thrust through, and whoever is caught will fall by the sword" (Isaiah 13:15).

B. T. D. Smith suggests more kindly that it is perhaps not so much the expression of a desire for revenge as an example of "a tendency to depict in as dark colours as possible the final fate of the sinful, whether unbelieving Jew or faithless Christian"[6] (a tendency which may explain certain other passages as well).

But for the purposes of this book I shall consider the parable of the Pounds only as a story of venture capital.

Separated from the story of the nobleman, the plot of The Pounds is recognizably similar to that of The Talents, though with important variations both in details and in the lessons to be drawn. The lesson of The Talents, as usually expounded, is that God distributes his gifts unequally but it is within everyone's power to do equally well *in proportion to his original endowment*, and that is how we shall be judged on the last day. The lesson of The Pounds, as usually expounded, is that we all have an equal opportunity, in some sense, and shall be rewarded *in proportion to our actual achievements*. There is also a striking difference in the fate of the slothful servant, in the two parables.

In the older commentaries, therefore, almost every chapter on this theme began with a discussion of whether The Talents and The Pounds were to be considered as two equally authentic stories—or authentic variants—told by Jesus, or as later variations developed by others from a single original story. The conservative verdict—the only possible verdict, unless one was prepared to challenge the Scriptural text—was that Jesus spoke both versions. According to the Gospel accounts they were told at different times and to different audiences—The Pounds to the multitude as Jesus travelled toward Jerusalem (Luke) and The Talents to the disciples alone on the Mount of Olives (Matthew). Neither book gives both parables.

Biblical scholars now, however, generally believe that in the transmission of the stories orally, through perhaps many narrators, the time and place of telling were not always preserved, and Matthew and Luke, working independently of each other, simply put them into their records at what seemed appropriate points. If so, time and place of telling are no longer proof of two stories, and the relationship must be determined strictly by internal evidence.

Although some commentators hold out for two independent parables as told by Jesus, the weight of opinion at present seems to be that Talents and Pounds are variants of a single original story. If so, what was that story?

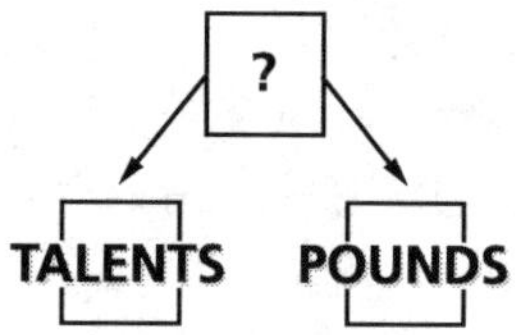

There is enough similarity in the versions so that it would seem quite feasible, allowing for some distortions with the passage of time, to discover the basic plan. In general usage details of the stories are often interchanged, the outstanding example of this being the "talent wrapped in a napkin."[7] In the two gospel versions, the talent (a large mass of coins) was buried in the earth; the pound (a handful) was merely tied up in a cloth and laid away. But early in church history the talent somehow took unto itself the napkin as a burial shroud, and in this garb it has haunted us ever since. In fact, the "talent in the napkin" has had such long usage and in such lofty circles that it must be accepted as traditional, and may be taken to represent the melding of the two parables in the public mind.

A similar tendency towards amalgamation is revealed when the talents are referred to in the same context as the king and his judgements (a fairly frequent error, especially in older authors), or when the numbers (of talents or pounds) are swapped between stories, or when the words "talents" and "pounds" themselves are interchanged. Some of this confusion, or conflation, reflects the fact that over the centuries the word "talent" has come to be the dominant word, standing for the capital in general, while "pound" is often thought of simply as a variant; and some confusion has been brought about deliberately in efforts to reconcile the stories. Thus a modern expositor can write, "In the parable of the pounds each man receives one talent."[8]

Yet the obstacles remain. The stories are close, but have never been brought any closer, and no one, so far as I know, has come forward with a prototype for a single, original parable as told by Jesus.[9]

There is another possibility, which I find the most likely. Adolph von Harnack, in *The Sayings of Jesus*, suggested that the parable of The Talents, as we know it, may have arisen from a combination of parables, but his two parables differ from those mentioned by Bruce. In Harnack's suggestion there is no lost parable of a king but two quite practical stories of delegated duties. In one the departing lord delivers his household to the care of his servants; in the other he gives them property (money) so that they may develop it.[10] Harnack felt that such an interweaving of plots had taken place in several cases, and says, "How this came to pass in the course of tradition it is no longer possible to discover," but in this case, at least, we can sketch a possible scenario.

In this hypothesis, one parable is The Servants Left in Charge, the other is The Pounds—both of them stories told by Jesus. At some point, I believe, these two stories were braided together by narrators, producing a composite story which we know as the Parable of the Talents.

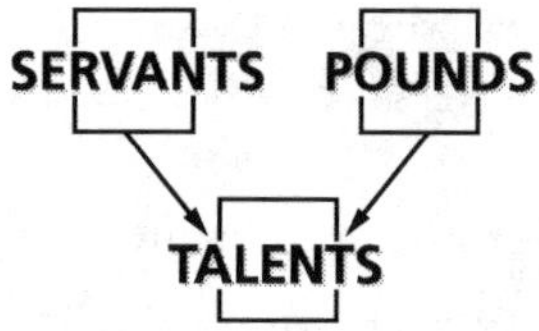

If the parable of the Servants Left in Charge does not sound familiar, it is because its existence as a complete parable might itself be called a hypothesis—but a strong one. The putative parable, as presented below, is made up of separate passages, apparently fragments of the same story, found in three different gospels and connected only by the situation described and the aptness of the conclusion.

The name is taken from the passage in Mark which opens the story. This passage is often called The Doorkeeper or The Watchman; the RSV calls it The Servants Left in Charge. I will use the last phrase as a name for the whole story, but I quote the text mainly as in the King James Version, because I believe that certain parts of it have been used in constructing what we know as The Talents, and keeping to that version makes it easier to see the relationship.

An Attempted Reconstruction of The Servants Left in Charge

> It is like a man taking a far journey, who left his house and gave authority to his servants, and to every man his work (Mark 13:34a KJV), according to his several ability, and straightway took his journey (Matt. 25:15b KJV).

No clues are left as to the nature of the work, which is probably in a large household or on a large estate, as in other parables. When the master returns, two of the servants, evidently the lesser ones, present their reports, and each in turn receives the master's praise:

> Well done, good and faithful servant. Thou hast been faithful over a few things. I will set thee over many things[11]—enter thou into the joy of thy lord (Matt.25:23 KJV).

This passage now forms part of the parable of the Talents, but it does not fit well there. "A few things!" The first two servants in The Talents had each been entrusted with a fortune! The master's commendation surely comes from the original tale of the Servants Left in Charge, and refers to duties rather than to money.

The probable conclusion of the story appears in both Matthew and Luke in passages variously called The Servant in Authority, The Faithful and Wise Steward, or The Faithful and Unfaithful Servants. These passages, apparently two slightly different versions of the same fragment, are not presented in either gospel as part of a narrative but are worked into a kind of sermon on the sudden coming of judgment. Nevertheless they give the impression of being part of a story—the story, in fact, of The Servants Left in Charge.

It is evident from the verses already quoted that the third servant in that story must be the one of highest rank, and also that he is destined to be the "horrible example."

Jesus first describes an ideal steward, then contrasts him with a corrupt steward who takes advantage of the master's absence.

> Who then is a faithful and wise servant [faithful and wise steward: Luke], whom his lord hath made ruler over his household, to give them meat in due season? Blessed is that servant, whom his lord when he cometh shall find so doing. Verily I say unto you, That he shall make him ruler over all his goods.

> But and if that evil servant shall say in his heart, My lord delayeth his coming; and shall begin to smite his fellow servants, and to eat and drink with the drunk-

> en; the lord of that servant shall come in a day when he looketh not for him, and in an hour that he is not aware of, and shall cut him asunder, and appoint him his portion with the hypocrites: there shall be weeping and gnashing of teeth (Matt. 24:45-51 KJV, Luke 12:42-48, KJV).

The phrase "cut him asunder" (*dichotomesei auton*, also translated as "cut him in half," "cut him in pieces," or simply "punish him") has given rise to many interesting footnotes, but judging from the context, what is meant here is simply "cut him off" (from the rest of the household); in other words, "cast him out."

This, followed by the "weeping and gnashing of teeth," is the very fate of the slothful servant in the parable of the Talents.

Luke's version of this passage concludes with a summarizing verse:

> For unto whom much is given, of him shall be much required: and to whom men have committed much, of him they will ask the more (Luke 12:48b KJV).

It is impossible to be sure whether these passages, taken from three different gospels, are all part of the same parable; but the basic situation in each is the same, and the last verse, with its clearly implied comparison of those who have been given much responsibility and those who have been given less ("each according to his ability") supplies a logical ending to The Servants Left in Charge, and appears to be that ending.

An important point to be noted is that this parable does not deal with money at all.

The other parable, however, The Pounds, is about money, and this may be a good place to bring up the subject.

Some Money Talk

It is often stated in discussions such as this that the value of the coins is not important, but the relative values are, as they throw much light on the logic and probable form of the original story. The form of the currency is also important, since it too influences interpretation.

The talent (*talanton*)[12] was originally a measure of weight: in modern equivalents about 114 pounds troy weight, or 94 pounds avoirdupois. (In the book of Revelation, where the King James Version speaks of "hailstones about the weight of a talent," the Revised Standard Version says "heavy as a hundredweight.") When large sums of money had to be handled, involving, as it often did in the East, currencies from many different countries, it was simpler to weigh the coins than to try to calculate equivalents: a mixed bag of silver coins weighing 94 pounds was simply "a talent of silver." The collection might even include lumps or articles of silver. By Jesus' time, however, the talent had been standardized in terms of coinage as 60 *minas*—rendered into English, by analogy with English currency, as "pounds."

But the New Testament "pound," like the talent, could be either a unit of weight—about a pound and a half in our English foot-pound system—or a sum of money: 50 shekels. The shekel was the largest coin in common use; it varied in weight from place to place and from century to century, but the shekel of Jesus' time seems to have been about the weight of an American half-dollar; fifty of them would make up more or less the weight of the old original "pound."

In the parable, one might think of the pound as five stacks of ten shekels each, which each servant scooped up and put into a purse, or—in the case of the third servant—tied up in a cloth. In sermons and other discussions of the parable the coins are sometimes referred to as gold (the monetary system did include gold shekels), but most of the coins in circulation were of silver, and both parables, in referring to the "money" use the word *argurion*, silver.

It seems to me that erroneous impressions of what the talent and the pound really were have been misleading interpreters for centuries. In the parable of the Pounds, each man's share was "equal" in the book-keeping sense: one pound; but it was not a single gift of some magical, mystical power or blessing conferred on all alike. On the contrary, as Jesus' hearers would have understood, the 50 coins entrusted to each man represented multiple opportunities for each one to try out his own ideas, to explore, to create, to win—and of course, to lose. In the parable of the Talents, the difference is merely that the amounts are much larger and are unequally distributed.

As the centuries passed and practical knowledge of Biblical times faded out, most hearers or readers would naturally think of the talent and the pound as single coins. When the parables were expounded, the "oneness" of the pound, as contrasted with the varied numbers of talents, became an important element in the interpretation, and so it has remained, to most interpreters, up to the present time.

As to the actual value of the coins, it is not possible to give good modern equivalents because of changing conditions over the ages, but it is possible, of course, to give a nominal value on the basis of the market price of silver at a given time and place. A figure frequently stated for the *mina* or pound in sermons and commentaries, until quite recent times, was about four pounds sterling or (at an outdated exchange rate) about 21 American dollars.[13] This seems to have been worked out at some time in the 19th century and to have been repeated uncritically ever since, in spite of its obvious lack of realism. (The text of Luke calls it "a very little," which has helped to perpetuate the impression that it was a trifle, but that must be an exaggeration of littleness for the sake of effect, just as Matthew exaggerates in the opposite direction.)

Recent works give a much higher estimate. At present-day rates and using the same method, the silver in the pound would be worth at least a hundred dollars. That is better, but a still more realistic idea of its value can be obtained by considering that one New Testament pound equated to a hundred denarii, and one denarius, as we know from another parable, was a day's pay for a laborer, so that the pound represented about four months' pay for a laboring man. Say that the daily wage was ten dollars in today's money: that would be considered high in some countries today, low in others; it is an arbitrary figure, but it is a thinkable one, and multiplied by 100 working days, it brings the pound out at a thousand dollars, a figure at which it seems very possible to go into a business venture.

Applying the same scale to Matthew's version of the story, one talent (60 pounds) would equate to $60,000, and the total amount left with the servants would be almost half a million dollars. (Some authorities would consider this conservative.)

An Attempted Reconstruction of The Pounds

Now to the parable of The Pounds. Below I give, freely expressed, a version of it as it might have run when it was new—only very much shortened, of course, because much of the story has been lost, and attention is fixed only on the dramatic denouement.

> A certain man went into a far country and before departing called in three of his servants and gave each man one pound and said to them, "See what you can do with this while I am away."
>
> When he returned he ordered the servants to whom he had given the money to be called to him so that he might know what they had gained by their efforts.
>
> The first man said, "Sir, your pound has made five pounds more." The master was delighted. The second man's profit was only two pounds, but the master was also happy with that. Both men were praised and

> promoted to greater responsibilities.
>
> Then the third man came forward, saying, "Sir, I knew you were a hard man and would have my hide if I lost the money, and frankly, I just didn't feel I was ready to act on my own. But I've kept your money safe—and here it is!"
>
> The master was astounded. "Why, you lazy good-for-nothing! So I'm a hard man, am I, and you're scared to death of me! If you had really been afraid you would have been out there working day and night to have something to show me. The truth is, *you thought I was an easy man!* You thought you could forget my interests and get by without making any effort. But you have been cheating me every day, wasting the time with nothing to show for it. Throw this man out; there's no room for him here!"

It would be the height of arrogance to suggest such changes in the Scriptural text if it did not appear that the story as Jesus told it had already been altered long ago, and probably more than once; but in the belief that such alterations were made, and that it is possible to go "behind" them and get somewhat closer to the original story, I will take up these suspected alterations one by one and try to defend my reconstructed version.

The first step in trying to bring the parable back to its original form is to replace "nobleman" (*anthropos tis eugenes*) with the simple word "man" (*anthropos*), which is how many of the parables begin ("A certain man… "). It is sometimes suggested that the traveller in Luke's story was a merchant and the "servants" were employees or assistants in his business. That would be logical, but all the other parables have a country setting, and the "power figure" in them is the landowner. So

I have stayed with "man."

Then I have changed the arithmetical figures back to what I believe is their proper place. The story of the Servants Left in Charge did not deal with money at all, so if my basic theory is correct, these figures must have come from the parable of The Pounds; and since in that parable all were given the same capital to begin with, the five, two and zero can only represent the *profits made by the servants.*[14]

When the two parables—Servants and Pounds—were combined to form The Talents, the figures five, two, and one were used to represent the varying sums given to the servants, but the basic formula (five-two-zero) surely came from Jesus himself. These are not the trite and mechanical "fives" and "tens" which beset this subject—both in the parables themselves, as recorded, and in the commentaries on them—but a modest and realistic spread which sounds true to life. The man who made five hundred percent is exceptional and represents the over-achievers, the brilliant or lucky few, and the man who made two hundred represents the modestly successful; but the profits are not multiples—people do not succeed so neatly in multiples of each other; they are simply points on a continuum which allows for any number of other possible points along it.

THE RECKONING

But of course the climax of the story is the scene between master and servant at the reckoning, and here I have departed most widely from the "script." I believe, on the grounds explained below, that the last six verses, from verse 22 to the end, were either added or altered later by unknown hands.

What made the servant answer as he did, when he might have been expected to apologize or explain or beg for another chance? He was afraid to risk the money, he said, but he was not afraid to insult his master to his face, and his characterization of him is blatantly insulting. The master's reply is equally strange, as with heavy sarcasm he accepts the charge and turns it against the servant ("Out of thine own mouth will I judge thee, thou wicked servant!") and then upbraids him for not having put the money in the bank, so that it would bring in some "usury," some interest.

The word "usury" as used in the King James Version meant simply "interest," without its modern connotation of "exorbitant interest," "exploitation." For many centuries this verse was the subject of a dispute centering on the fact that Old Testament law did not allow the taking of interest from one's fellows, and this taboo was maintained by Christians, in theory at least, through the Middle Ages and almost to modern times. Did Jesus sanction "usury"? Modern scholarship, however, tells us that that part of Jewish law dated from a time when the Hebrews were almost entirely a pastoral and agricultural people, and the loans envisioned were not for business use but to assist the poor who in hard times might otherwise be compelled to sell themselves as slaves. Such loans were really acts of charity, not commercial transactions. By Jesus' time commerce had increased to the point where making loans and taking interest on them was a common business practice.

But was the reference to interest even a part of the original parable? Jesus usually drove home his points in the strongest possible terms. To make such a feeble ending, to offer loopholes or suggest halfway measures, was not his style. This passage sounds like the work of a later narrator, offering a more comfortable, more people-pleasing ending to the story; it implies that if the third servant had simply put the money in the bank and let it draw interest, that might have been acceptable service. It is an implication that has always puzzled interpreters, since it seems to defeat the whole point of the story.

Was the third servant really afraid, or was he merely lazy? The parable of the Pounds does not use the word but makes the point indirectly with the detail of the "napkin"—a large handkerchief used to wipe away sweat. The man had just been given a chunk of cash—not a trifling amount, as often supposed, but a sizeable advance of his master's money. The fifty coins had to be kept in something, and a bandana would have been a handy, if somewhat unprofessional, expedient, so he tied them up in the "sweatcloth" as a temporary purse, and put them away. He did not bury them, for he probably thought of doing something with them… some day… when the perfect opportunity offered. There is irony in the lazy man's use of a sweatcloth, but the real significance of the detail is that (a) he was very casual about his duties, and (b) he cannot have been afraid of his master, since he took so little pains to protect his property.

In spite of that, innumerable expositors have seized upon the line, "I feared thee, because thou art an austere man," and have launched into sermons on the subject of fear, arguing that the servant's error was to see his master in his own narrow and wicked likeness, etc., etc. This is the most common explanation of the servant's attitude, but a rarer and I think a far more plausible one is suggested in an 1898 sermon by British clergyman Canon Winterbotham (and adopted in my reconstruction):

> One thing only seems to detract from the wonderful effectiveness of the parable. The wicked and slothful servant is represented, somewhat elaborately, as acting as he does under the influence of fear and dislike. At any rate that is the excuse he makes, and the excuse is not declared to be false. On the contrary it is accepted as true, and shown to be a reason for the greater carefulness. Now it is the universal conviction that the "unprofitable servant" neglects his Master's interests almost always out of idleness, indifference, self-indulgence—not out of dislike or fear… *The disposition to presume upon our Lord's goodness has always been incalculably stronger than the disposition to exaggerate His severity.*[15] [Italics added]

The last statement strikes me as the most logical explanation of the servant's behavior that I have heard, and the most true to human nature in general.

I must differ, however, on another point. Canon Winterbotham is obviously unconvinced by the servant's excuse, which flies in the face of his own experience, and according to him, of "universal conviction," but since, in the parable, it is accepted, he does not press the point. He merely says, "That servant does not seem to be drawn from real life." I think the servant was drawn from real life and was running true to form; he is the man who never makes an effort but always has an excuse, and now, caught in a tight spot, he is simply trying to lie his way out of it.

It is the master, in this parable, who is not drawn from real life. He not only accepts the preposterous excuse and the insults, he even points out how the servant might have got by without any real effort! In real life, if the master had been satisfied to have the money left with the bankers he would have left it there himself; there was no point in involving his employees. He had left the money with them specifically to be used in trade, used "creatively," we might say; he would have been dumbfounded if the third servant had produced a passbook in lieu of a profit.

The easy way out—just putting the money in the bank to draw interest—sounds like a concession offered by later expounders. Jesus, who told the original story, usually drove home his points in the strongest possible terms. To make such a feeble ending—to offer loopholes or suggest halfway measures, as here—was not his way.

Finally, there is the transfer of the lazy servant's pound to the diligent one.

> He said unto them that stood by, "Take from him the pound, and give it to him that hath ten pounds" (Luke 19:24 KJV).

Was this transaction a part of the story as Jesus told it, or was it added later, along with the saying, "Unto every one that hath shall be given"? That saying occurs in three other places in the gospels in completely different contexts (Matt. 13:12, Mark 4:25, Luke 8:18), so it was not, at least, uniquely inspired by this parable. In fact it seems pointless here, since the capital never belonged to the servants but was at all times the property of the master, along with the profits derived from it; the taking of the money from one servant and the handing of it to another could not have been either punishment for the one or reward for the other, except in terms of "face."

A supposition that the transfer of funds was a later addition to the story is strengthened by the fact that it leaves the second servant without a bonus, though by the logic of the saying he deserved one just as much as the first.

If this bit was added, why was it added? One explanation, offered by Joachim Jeremias and others, is that there was a tendency on the part of the early church to add extra conclusions to the stories in the form of generalizing *logia*, or sayings. "We are not in any way calling in question the authenticity of the logia themselves," said Jeremias, "but only insisting that they were not originally uttered as the conclusion of a parable... By employing them in this way it was intended to give the parables the widest possible application."[16] As a general observation this offers a helpful explanation of the puzzling conclusions found in connection with many parables. Here, it is suggested, the transfer of the useless servant's pound to the useful one is simply some early editor's device for attaching this saying.

A suggestion that seems more persuasive in this case, however, is that the transfer was introduced into The Pounds for the specific purpose of filling a need in the plot.[17] By this point in the story Luke's version is pressing on toward the condemnation of the disloyal citizens, an event which, with the introduction of the kingly theme, has become the real climax of the parable. The hostile citizens are duly punished, by being slain; but what should be done about the slothful servant, a member of the king's own household? His crime is not so great as theirs, yet it is clearly necessary to mete out some punishment. The "wicked servant" cannot be allowed to go scot-free; and so he is given a symbolic slap on the wrist, and justice is served.

Strange to say, this punishment also appears in The Talents, even though it is not needed there, where the slothful servant is simply fired. But the narrator could not resist adding this detail, or perhaps he was afraid to omit it, lest it turn out to have a hidden significance.

How did these elements from the two older parables come to combine, not very smoothly, into a new story, The Talents? Perhaps in the course of many retellings these two parables, with their similar tales of absent masters, gradually became intermingled. Or perhaps—and I think more probably—some well-meaning narrator deliberately introduced the money theme from The Pounds into the tale of The Servants, because money is always a catchier theme than duty, and he hoped to combine the best of both yarns. He saw that distributing the money unequally, "to each according to his ability," provided a more intriguing beginning than the flat distribution of The Pounds, and seemed more true to life. Everywhere, in every age, some people do start out with more advantages than others; this is a situation that we all recognize and wonder about, and so the audience is captured from the start.

The transformation of the prosaic pounds into the dazzling talents—a simple enough device available to all tellers of symbolic tales—made the story still more attractive. In fact, the development of the composite story, once the money has been made a part of it, is dominated by the money theme, except for the master's praise of the good servants. They had been told to trade, with the aim, of course, of making a profit, and they had done so, successfully. But the praise is only for their faithfulness. This sounds somewhat inadequate. They were not, it seems, simply carrying on an established business, where faithfulness would be enough to bring success; they had been challenged to launch out on their own, which would require imagination, initiative, energy, and often daring. But in the master's commendation there is no recognition of those qualities. The story-teller has retained the original wording found in The Servants Left in Charge.

There are several reasons for offering this version of The Pounds, flawed as it may be.

First, it is generally assumed that the merchant's purpose in entrusting money to three different men was not only to keep it active in his absence, but also to test their competence. If the money had been distributed, as Matthew says, "to each according to his ability," it would have meant that the master already knew their abilities and did not need such a test; it would also mean that he was playing favorites, since "it takes money to make money." If the purpose was to test the employees, it would be logical to start them all out even.

Second, this would answer a much-discussed question: why did Jesus make the one-talent man (in Matthew's version) the loser? We know that Jesus had great sympathy for the underdog. He could just as well have made the five-talent or the two-talent man the hoarder, while the one-talent man came through as a winner because, though he had little, he put that little to good use. That the story does not run that way strengthens the theory that in the original parable there was no "underdog," because there was no difference in the amounts of money entrusted. There were just three men who had equal opportunity, but one of them chose not to use it.

(In The Talents the association of the third servant's laziness with the smallness of his capital has become so familiar that expositors sometimes have to stop and remind us that the two have no intrinsic connection: sloth is just as likely to afflict the well-endowed as the humble. The parable of the Pounds is free of this distracting feature.)

Third, although the "diversity of gifts" seems more true to life and is the reason why that version is so popular, it doesn't work out as well for teaching purposes. When the time comes to compare the servants' results they are not comparable, because the men started out with such different sums. The story-teller could of course use any figure he wished as the second servant's profit, but that would mean introducing another variable into the picture, and the parable would become simply a kind of fairy-tale about individuals. Matthew's solution avoids that by setting the second man's profit at the same ratio to his capital as the first man's, thus making him equally successful, but that blunts one of the main points of the story. It is only when all the men begin with the same capital but end with different results that the significance of the master's appraisal becomes apparent.

This means setting up an artificial example, because in life no two people begin exactly equal. And that, I think, explains the parable of The Pounds. It is not intended to represent life as a whole, much less our different lots; it is a textbook case, a hypothetical situation designed to illustrate one point: that just as the worldly owner who looks for profit will accept varying results, depending on circumstances, but will not tolerate apathy, so God expects us to be active and creative in his behalf.

When the parable of the Pounds was first told that must have been clear, but as the parable of the Talents began to circulate, with its more elaborate plot suggesting the inequality of human gifts, both parables came to be interpreted much more broadly. That the two stories as they circulated influenced each other and in fact copied from each other is apparent; and the end of the process was that both came to be seen as symbolic, though conflicting, representations of the way our earthly lot is determined.

Eventually the composite version became so much more famous than either of its sources that the story of the Pounds, like that of the Servants, might have dropped out of circulation altogether (except—

probably, and ironically—for the presence in it of that controversial figure, the nobleman).

But the story called "The Talents" survived and flourished.

End of Part One

Intermission

Now, having set forth in some detail the conclusions, right or wrong, to which my study has led me, I must put those conclusions on the shelf for a while and ask the reader to do the same. The search for the original form of the parable will always be worthwhile, and I do not apologize for spending some time on it, but it is not the primary concern of this book, as will be evidenced in Part Two (in progress). That concern is to determine, so far as possible, the impact upon Christians of the parable as it is recorded in the gospels and as it has been preached for twenty centuries. For whatever speculation may be made as to the exact form of the lesson, the heart of it remains unchanged, with the same mixture of warning, encouragement and mystery that it has always had.

Something of value—some capital—has been given to each of us to trade with; woe to those who take this trust too lightly! That is the warning.

Whole-hearted effort will be rewarded, regardless of apparent results; that is the encouragement.

As for the capital: that is a mystery which everyone must solve for himself.

Notes

Notes for Chapter 1: In Search of an Ethic

1. Max Weber first published *Die protestantische Ethik und der Geist des Kapitalismus* (The Protestant Ethic and the Spirit of Capitalism) as a two-part article in 1904-05, in the *Archiv für Sozialwissenschaft und Sozialpolitick.* The original version was put into English by Talcott Parsons in 1930. In 1958 Parsons issued a new translation based on the expanded version which had appeared in *Gesammelte Aufsätze zur Religionssociologie* (Collected Essays on the Sociology of Religion), 1920-21. All citations in this book are from the 1958 edition, published by Charles Scribner's Sons, New York.
2. Weber, p.181.
3. Weber, p. 35.
4. Weber, pp. 48, 49. Here he is quoting Benjamin Franklin, *Works*, Sparks Edition, Vol. 2, p. 87ff.
5. Weber, p. 51.
6. Weber, p. 53.
7. Weber, p. 180. Franklin was not a Puritan or even a Christian. Though his background was Protestant (Congregationalist), he himself was a Deist. Weber felt that this fact, far from damaging his argument, strengthened it, since it showed how strongly the "ethic" persisted even when the religious convictions that created it had lapsed.
8. Weber, p. 17.

9. Weber, p. 17.
10. Weber, p. 80.
11. Weber, pp. 176, 177.
12. Weber, p. 54.
13. William Safire, *Before the Fall: An Inside View of the Pre-Watergate White House*, Garden City, N.Y., Doubleday & Co., Inc. 1975, p. 582.
14. Baltimore *Sun*, Letters to the Editor, June 9, 1979.
15. Letter and reply, *The Washington Post*, July 22, 1983, p. 64.
16. Letter and reply, Tampa *Tribune*, October 16, 1983, p. 7-I.
17. Weber, p. 115.
18. Paul Tillich, *A History of Christian Thought*, edited by Carl E. Braaten, SCM Press Ltd., London, 1968, pp. 225, 226.
19. Max Weber, *The Sociology of Religion*, Boston, Beacon Press, 1963, pp. 95, 253. First published in Germany in 1922 by J. C. B. Mohr (Paul Siebeck) as *Religions Soziologie*. On page 270 of the same work Weber refers to Jesus as "primarily a magician whose magical charisma was an ineluctable source of his unique feeling of individuality."
20. Weber, *Prot. Ethic*, pp. 83, 84.
21. *Ibid.*, p. 163.
22. John Milton, "The Reason of Church-Governement urg'd against Prelaty," *The Works of John Milton*, Vol. 3, Part One, New York, Columbia University Press, 1931, p. 229.
23. John Milton, "When I consider how my light is spent" (sonnet), *Complete Poetry and Selected Prose of John Milton,* New York, The Modern Library, 1950, pp. 530-531.
24. Cotton Mather, *Bonifacius, An Essay Upon the Good,* ed. by David Levin, Cambridge, The Belknap Press of Harvard University Press, 1966, p. 119. Henry Jeanes was an English Puritan clergyman. Levin's note says he was considered a witty and practical writer on religious questions.
25. Richard Steele, *The Tradesman's Calling*, London, printed by J. D. for S. Sprint, 1684, p. 9. Steele was a minister but was best known

for his work on "the right management of the tradesman's calling." The book was popular for more than 70 years.

26. Rita F. Snowden, *Such a Woman*, London, The Epworth Press, 1963, p. 31. Susannah was the mother of John and Charles Wesley, founders of Methodism.
27. Letter to Thomas Butts, *The Complete Writings of William Blake*, ed. Geoffrey Keynes, London, Oxford University Press, 1966, pp. 812, 813.

Notes for Chapter 2: Jesus the Steward

1. *Webster's New Twentieth Century Dictionary*, Second Edition, 1975, William Collins + World Publishing Co., Inc.
2. Morris Goldstein, *Jesus in the Jewish Tradition*, New York, The Macmillan Company, 1950, pp. 113, 114.
3. The word *oikonomos* (pronounced "ēkonómos") is derived from *oikía,* "house," as are several other words important in this chapter: *oikonomía* (stewardship, management), *oikodespótes* ("owner" or "steward" of a house) and *oikétes* ("servant, houseboy"). The syllable which begins all these words is pronounced as "long e," so *oikonomia* becomes *"ēkonomía,"* etc.
4. *The Interpreter's Bible*, New York, Abingdon Press, 1952, Vol. 7, p. 727.
5. George M. Lamsa, *Gospel Light, Comments on the Teachings of Jesus from Aramaic and Unchanged Eastern Customs*, Revised Edition, A. T. Holman Company, Philadelphia, 1939, pp. 180, 181.
6. It may be inferred from this passage that Jesus' mother, like his brothers, was no longer in Nazareth. She appears, however, in the story of the wedding at Cana, a nearby town (John 2:1-11). Possibly one of the brothers had established himself in Cana, and Mary, the widowed mother, lived in his household. If the wedding involved a member of that family then Mary's concern over the

arrangements, and her authority with the servants, would be understandable.

7. Richard A. Batey, "Sepphoris, An Urban Portrait of Jesus," *Biblical Archaeology Review*, May/June 1992, Vol. 18, No. 3, p. 52.
8. Batey, p. 52.
9. Eric Meyers, quoted in "Ancient Sepphoris: Portrait of a Cosmopolitan City," by Angela M. H. Schuster, *Archaeology*, March/April 1997, p. 64. The same article contains the following information:

> Founded ca. 800 B.C., Sepphoris became an important center of Hebrew learning by the first century A.D. Here, according to the Jewish historian Flavius Josephus, Rabbi Judah Ha-Nasi the Patriarch compiled the Mishnah, the authoritative body of Jewish law on which the Talmud is based. Christian pilgrims, believing Sepphoris to be the birthplace of Saints Anne and Joachim, parents of the Virgin Mary, flocked to the city until the end of the Crusader period. Sepphoris played a vital role in the trade between the port of Acre (ancient Akko) and the fertile Jezreel and Beth-Shean valleys. Its central location in the richest area of southern Galilee also made it an important outpost of the Roman and Byzantine empires. The site was continuously inhabited until 1948, when the Arab village of Saffuriyeh was razed during Israel's war of independence.

10. This is made clear in recent translations, which use the specific word "reclining," as in the Greek text, whereas older versions used "sitting at table" ("sitting at meat").
11. Luke 12:36,37. This last example probably depicts the master distributing to his servants some of the take-home treats provided at the wedding.

12. Liddell and Scott, *A Greek-English Lexicon, With a Supplement*, Oxford, Clarendon Press, 1996. Of course to make the point we must assume that Jesus quoted the remark, or at least the key word, in Greek.
13. *The Interpreter's Bible,* New York, Abingdon Press, 1952, Vol. 8, p. 556.
14. Alfred Marshall, *The Interlinear Greek-English New Testament*, Second Edition, Grand Rapids, Michigan, Zondervan Publishing House, 1976. I have also used *The New Greek Interlinear New Testament*, 1990, edited by J. D. Douglas and published by Tyndale House Publishers, Inc., Wheaton, Illinois.

NOTES FOR CHAPTER 3: STEWARDSHIP AS A RECURRING THEME

1. The classic example of allegorical interpretation, and the one always brought out to illustrate the method, is St. Augustine's treatment of the parable of The Good Samaritan (Luke 10:30-37):

    A certain man went down from Jerusalem to Jericho; Adam himself is meant; *Jerusalem* is the heavenly city of peace, from whose blessedness Adam fell; *Jericho* means the moon, and signifies our mortality, because it is born, waxes, wanes, and dies. *Thieves* are the devil and his angels. *Who stripped him*, namely, of his immortality; *and beat him*, by persuading him to sin; *and left him half-dead,* because in so far as man can understand and know God, he lives, but in so far as he is wasted and oppressed by sin, he is dead; he is therefore called *half-dead.* The *priest* and *Levite* who saw him and passed by, signify the priesthood and ministry of the Old Testament, which could profit

> nothing for salvation. *Samaritan* means Guardian, and therefore the Lord himself is signified by this name. The *binding of the wounds* is the restraint of sin. *Oil* is the comfort of good hope; *wine* the exhortation to work with fervent spirit. The *beast* is the flesh in which He deigned to come to us. The being *set upon the beast* is the belief in the incarnation of Christ. The *inn* is the Church, where travellers returning to their heavenly country are refreshed after pilgrimage. The *morrow* is after the resurrection of the Lord. The *two pence* are either the two precepts of love, or the promise of this life and of that which is to come. The *innkeeper* is the Apostle (Paul). The supererogatory payment is either his counsel of celibacy, or the fact that he worked with his own hands lest he should be a burden to any of the weaker brethren when the Gospel was new, though it was lawful for him "to live by the Gospel."

This passage appears in many works on allegory; I have copied it from C. H. Dodd, who notes that it comes from *Quaestiones Evangeliorum*, II, 19—slightly abridged. C. H. Dodd, *The Parables of the Kingdom*, New York, Charles Scribner's Sons, 1961, pp. 1, 2. Some allegorical interpretations of the Parable of the Talents are seen in Chapter 5 of this book.

2. Richard L. Rohrbaugh, "A Peasant Reading of the Parable of the Talents/Pounds: A Text of Terror?", Jamaica, N.Y., *Biblical Theology Bulletin), 23* (1993), p. 37.
3. The fact that salt never loses its taste has caused much discussion of these verses. If the original word had been "spice" that would have fitted the context better, as spice does lose its flavor all too quickly. But all three gospels say "salt."
4. Because I believe that Jesus knew at first hand just how much

work a "company dinner" was, I reject the usual interpretation of his famous remark to Martha: "You are anxious and troubled about many things; one thing is needful. Mary has chosen the good portion, which shall not be taken away from her" (Luke 10:38-42). He knew that even in the best-organized household nothing comes by itself, and if Martha stopped working nobody would be fed; but he also knew that work can become a tyrant, leaving no time for reflection, and he spoke as a friend, to liberate her. ("Martha, you are wearing yourself out with all this; we don't need so many dishes; one would be enough.") By implication he invited her to cut down the "much serving" and follow her sister's example; and this story is her grateful recollection of that day.

5. This version then goes on, in a puzzling non-sequitur that may originally have come from another parable (Matt. 22:11-14). It is irrelevant here.
6. Ernest Renan, *Life of Jesus* (Eng. trans.), New York, A. L. Burt, n.d., p. 186.
7. S. Parks Cadman, *Life of Jesus*, Philadelphia, David McKay Company, 1931, p. 17.
8. Roderic Dunkerley, *Beyond the Gospels*, London, Whitefriars Press, Ltd., Penguin Books, 1957, reprinted 1961, p.142.
9. Dunkerley, p. 153.
10. Dunkerley, pp. 153, 154.
11. Dunkerley, p. 85.
12. Adolf Hausrath, *Neutestamentliche Zeitgeschichte* (A History of New Testament Times), Vol. 1, Trans. by Williams and Norgate, London, L. Huxley, 1895, pp.188, 189. This extract is part of a footnote in *The Parabolic Teaching of Christ* by Alexander Balmain Bruce, Fourth Revised Edition, New York, Hodder & Stoughton, George H. Doran Company, 1886, pp. 243, 244.
13. J. B. Phillips, *The Gospels Translated into Modern English*, New York, The MacMillan Co., 1957, p. 242.

14. This is an agricultural watchtower. "These towers provided elevated positions from which fields were guarded; the ground floor of such structures served as living quarters for field workers or guards, since ripening crops had to be guarded day and night." *The Harper Collins Bible Dictionary*, Paul J. Achtempier, General Editor, Harper San Francisco, 1996, p. 1164.
15. Because of its possible connections with Jesus' occupation I have puzzled a good deal over the word *oikodespotes*, usually translated "householder," sometimes "housemaster," "landlord," etc. Liddell and Scott's *Greek-English Lexicon* says "master or steward of a house;" the supplement adds "master of an estate." In most of the parables the *oikodespotes* is clearly the master, but in this one he seems just as clearly to be the steward, who goes out early and late to hire workers for the vineyard that he manages for the *kyrios*, the owner. If one accepts that identification, the story becomes much clearer and there is no need to bring in an additional character (the *epitropos*, or foreman) to pay the workers. The steward has hired the workers, promising to pay them whatever is right, but when at the end of the day he pays them according to new instructions, the workers complain against him to the owner, who then speaks up to defend his decision.

Notes for Chapter 4: Talents and Pounds

1. Richard Chenevix Trench, *Notes on the Parables of Our Lord*, Ninth Edition, New York, D. Appleton & Co., 1857, p. 220.
2. Alexander Balmain Bruce, *The Parabolic Teaching of Christ*, Fourth Revised Edition, New York, Hodder & Stoughton, George H. Doran Company, 1886, pp. 216-217.
3. The Rev. J. G. Simpson, Canon of St. Paul's, "The Parable of the Pounds," in *The Expository Times*, September, 1926, p. 301.

4. *Parousia*, from the Greek for "presence" or "arrival" is used to refer to the second coming of Christ.
5. Luke Timothy Johnson, "The Lukan Kingship Parable (Lk. 19:11-27)," *Novum Testamentum*, Vol. 24, 2 (1982), pp. 139-159.
6. B. T. D. Smith, *The Parables of the Synoptic Gospels*, Cambridge, at the University Press, 1937, p. 163.
7. R. C. McQuilken issued a rare reminder to the modern reader that one should not speak of wrapping the talent in a napkin—an impossibility because of its mass and weight (*Studying Our Lord's Parables*, Grand Rapids, Michigan, Zondervan Publishing House, 1935, p. 99). (But, as O. Henry remarked in an unfinished story, any hotel man knows it is quite easy to wrap a *pound* of silver in a napkin. "The Unprofitable Servant," from *The Complete Works of O. Henry*, Garden City, New York, Garden City Publishing Co., 1937, p. 1007.)
8. George A. Buttrick, *Parables of Jesus*, Doubleday, Doran & Co., Garden City, New York, 1928, p. 244, note.
9. An exception, of sorts, to this statement is found in *The Nazarene Gospel Restored*, by Robert Graves, the poet and classical scholar, in collaboration with Joshua Podro (Cassell & Co., Ltd., London, 1953, pp. 338-343). Their version is really a radical rewrite which includes some features of both parables but tells a completely different story. Each servant receives one talent, but the main interest is in the story of the king and the citizens. The authors state that as a pious Jew dedicated to a life of poverty, Jesus could not have told this parable as we now have it, and that the servant who hid the talent rather than use it to support his master's capitalistic ventures must originally have been the hero, not the villain of the story. They assume that by "trading" the parable means using "usury and fraudulent wiles;" the servant who hid the talent was afraid to obey the king lest he offend against the religious law. In their version the wicked king and his nine wicked servants are

lynched by the citizens, while the righteous servant who refused to join them in "oppressing the people" is made a judge.

10. Adolph von Harnack, *The Sayings of Jesus: The Second Source of St. Matthew and St. Luke*, translated by the Rev. J. R. Wilkinson, London, Williams & Norgate, 1908, p. 125.
11. This is the literal translation, as given in Nestle and Marshall's *Interlinear Greek-English New Testament*. The KJV has "I will make thee ruler over many things"—perhaps influenced by Luke's "royal" version of the story; but this seems more appropriate here.
12. The information about the value of a talent in this paragraph of the text and the following two paragraphs comes mainly from *Harper's Bible Dictionary*, 1959; the *Dictionary of the Bible*, ed. James Hastings et al., 1963, Charles Scribner's Sons; and *The Expositor's Bible Commentary*, 1984, Zondervan Corporation, Grand Rapids, Michigan. The sources do not always agree in detail on this difficult subject, but are close enough for the purposes of this discussion.
13. Richard Chenevix Trench, a much quoted interpreter of the parables, may have been the source of this. A footnote on page 418 of his *Notes on the Parables of Our Lord*, 1857, gives the value of the New Testament pound as £4 1s 3d. At the exchange rate quoted for 1859 (B. R. Mitchell, *British Historical Statistics,* 1988, p. 702), that would be about $21 in American terms.
14. I base this conclusion not only on the construction of the story, as explained, but on the experience of reading so many expositions of it in which the "tyranny of ten" in the human mind is unmistakable. An amazingly high number of authorities err in quoting these famous figures, and most of the errors involve some combination of five and ten (occasionally five, three, and one). Jonathan Swift, for instance, says, "Some he hath trusted with one talent, some with five, and some with ten." This is a fairly common error, and the story itself is sometimes referred to as "the parable of the

ten talents" (though it starts with eight and ends with fifteen). The quest for symmetry, and the association of the number ten with perfection or completion, are so influential that famous scholars and preachers, with the written word lying on their desks, quote the numbers from memory, and get them wrong. If almost anyone else had told this story it would probably have said ten and five, but I believe five and two are the figures used by Jesus for the profit on the pounds, and then borrowed into The Talents as the varying "gifts" of capital.

15. Rayner Winterbotham, Canon of St. Mary's Cathedral, Edinburgh, *The Kingdom of Heaven Here and Hereafter*, London, 1898, p. 178.
16. Joachim Jeremias, *The Parables of Jesus*, SCM Press, Ltd., London, Study Edition, 1972, p.110.
17. This suggestion is not original with me. Unfortunately, I can no longer find the source of it.

The Talents

Index to Part One

The author spent most of her working years as a research analyst in the National Security Agency, from which she is now retired.

If you wish to contact her, write to:

Doris E. Miller
c/o Publishing Services, Inc.
8832 N Port Washington Rd #150
Milwaukee, WI 53217